DO WHAT YOU CAN!

Simple Steps — Extraordinary Results

JOHN J. HALL

Game Creek Publishing

Copyright © 2012 by John J. Hall.

Cover design and interior page layout by Kerrie Lian,
under contract with MacGraphics Services
Edited by Barbara McNichol, Barbara McNichol Editorial

Do What You Can! : simple steps — extraordinary results/
John Hall.—1st edition
Visit www.JohnHallSpeaker.com
Printed in the United States of America
First Printing: April 2012
ISBN: 978-0-9850727-0-4

1. Change—Personal and Business. 2. Success 3. Motivation

Library of Congress Control Number: 2012931778

The author and publisher endeavor to make the information in this
book accurate and up to date. It is a general guide. Before taking
action on medical, legal, or financial matters you should consult
with qualified professionals who can help you consider your unique
circumstances. The author and publisher cannot accordingly accept any
liability for any loss or damage suffered as a consequence of relying on
the information contained in this book.

Mention of specific leaders in research, education, therapy, or other
authorities in this book does not imply they endorse this book. Internet
addresses are accurate at the time of printing.

For my bride

KRISTINA

*Your courage, dedication and love
inspire me every single day.*

For my parents

HARRY S. and RUTH G. HALL

*Every day of their sixty-five years of married life together,
they simply got up and did what needed to be done.*

CONTENTS

TABLE OF

CONTENTS *(continued)*

TABLE OF

INTRODUCTION

Success in life is measured in many ways: accomplishment of business or artistic goals; recognition by professional peers; financial and personal security; providing a stable day-to-day environment for your family.

To me, success is largely measured by people's ability to identify their individual and collective purpose—their reason for being on earth—and living passionately in pursuit of that purpose.

Successful people make a point of doing both the many major and minor things that need to be done to live aligned with their purpose and goals. They know where they want to go in the short and long term, and they take action every day to make that happen. They start each day with a clear idea of what they need to do—and then do it.

My father is an example. A perpetually happy man, he knew his purpose and pursued it with passion. He took great pride in providing for his seven-member family through hard work and setting a responsible example for his children to follow. He brought that same energy and dedication to his job. Because of his efforts, as children we felt loved and secure, and as adults we pursued educational goals and careers of our choice.

One vivid image of my father's dedication has stayed with me all of these years. It's a beautiful June morning in 1966. With my brothers and sisters, I'm eating breakfast at the dining room table in our Philadelphia row house before heading off to school. My father comes down the stairs dressed in his dark suit—either blue or gray depending on the day—complete with a starched white shirt, glossy black shoes, and a navy blue tie.

He embraces us with his warm smile and says "good morning" as my mother sets his breakfast on the table. Eggs scrambled soft, black coffee, pink grapefruit, white toast. His pace is deliberate as he chews his food and asks each of us about our school assignments. When he's finished eating, he glances at his watch and pushes back his chair. After picking up his black briefcase and grey felt hat at the door, he gives my mother a loving kiss. Then he walks purposefully to the curb, climbs into his new blue Impala, a company car, and drives to his job as an insurance claims manager.

Day after day, year after year, my father's purpose and actions remained the same—doing everything he could for his family with immense skill, ceaseless energy, and deep passion. In short, he did what he could, with whatever he had available to him, right where he was in life. Because of that, my father was successful—and a big hero of mine.

Another hero of mine is Theodore "Teddy" Roosevelt, the twenty-sixth president of the United States. Roosevelt had a reputation for putting important ideas into simple language. He even inspired me to name a whole system *Do What You Can* with this one powerful quotation:

"Do what you can, with what you've got, where you are."

With a deep understanding of their life's purpose, both of my parents lived Roosevelt's mandate to "do what they could with what they had." Each day of their sixty-five years together, they consistently took small steps that led to success on their terms—always doing what they could for each other, their children, and their community. Providing crystal clear direction for me and my four siblings, they modeled how to live in a purposeful way. Through their lives—at every point of transition—they made major and minor decisions based on what they *knew* was important. In doing so, they also laid a strong foundation for decision-making in my own life and set an example for us all to follow.

LARGE-SCALE LIFE TRANSITIONS

Every day, you make a thousand minor transitions, mostly without conscious thought. You move through your day deciding where to go, what to eat, and how to spend your time.

Large-scale life changes also occur. Some of them are forced on you, such as illness, divorce, loss of employment, or death of loved ones. Major changes that are joyful arise, too, such as marriage, the birth or adoption of a child, graduations, promotions, retirement, even relocation to a place you've always wanted to live. Some large-scale transitions are marked by clear boundaries, such as leaving military service to return to civilian life. Others build gradually, such as when your children prepare to leave home to live independently.

Although this book touches on some of life's minor decisions, it mainly addresses major life transitions. Why? Because it's during these transitions that the need to set new goals becomes urgent. These decision times provide opportunities to consciously move from Point A to Point B and beyond.

If you're embroiled in a major change now, regard this as an excellent opportunity to pause, take stock, and ask, "What's next?" And if you believe you're here on earth for a special reason, this large-scale transitional time can move you more fully toward your purpose. Embrace this opportunity to clarify your goals and empower yourself to make them real!

But how? By applying the *Do What You Can System* or simply *The System*.

INTRODUCING *THE SYSTEM*

The system I've developed called the *Do What You Can System* supports you in discovering and pursuing your life's purpose, completely and without doubt or regret. As you follow this six-step system, you'll gain clarity in your goals and actions by exploring all three parts of Roosevelt's mandate: "Do what you can, with what you've got, where you are."

The System helps you clarify what you *want* to do and expand what you *can* do—wherever you are right now and wherever you wish to be—while applying an abundance of resources to achieve your goals. After working through its six steps, you'll be amazed at what you CAN do!

The System is based on my observations of successful people who know their purpose and live in alignment with it. They experience life on their own terms, often because they stopped doing what got in their way. Like my parents, these people get up each day and do the best they can with what they have. They hold a clear, steadfast idea of what they want and why it's important, then they work hard to achieve it.

Purposeful people get results while making our world a better place. They serve others while meeting their own obligations. They think, they dream, but most important, they *take action* that moves them in a meaningful direction.

Let's be clear: You don't *have to* make changes. However, you *are* responsible for the quality of your life. To achieve the degree of quality you want, decide what changes you want to make. What shifts are hiding in the back of your mind?

It's time to bring those thoughts of improvement to light, make them a priority, and turn them into reality. Yes, you *can* move from vague ideas to daily actions and a life filled with joy and purpose.

SIX ASSUMPTIONS

In creating this *Do What You Can System*, I've made the following six assumptions about you. Are these accurate for you at this time in your life?

1. *I assume you have an interest in truly achieving what you can and are willing to take specific actions to achieve your*

goals. The System isn't focused on changing the world, although that may indeed be your intention. Rather, it focuses on achieving daily, weekly, and long-term results that you want and believe are possible in your health, relationships, career, finances, and community.

2. *I assume you accept full responsibility for your results.* Although many people may help you and others may get in your way, over time, only you are responsible for who you are, what you do, and the results you obtain. If you're not ready to accept full responsibility for your results, your ability to realize your goals will be limited by what others permit you to do.

3. *I assume you sense a gap between what is and what could be, even though you may be reasonably content with where you are and the results you've achieved.* You feel you could close the gap if only you could (1) set a clear goal for what you want and (2) focus your efforts toward that goal. (In *The System,* you'll find step-by-step instructions and exercises on how to convert your life goals into effective daily behavior via *The System.)*

4. *I assume you're ready to build momentum and velocity.* In high school science class, we studied inertia—the tendency of a body at rest to remain at rest. We also learned about the power of *momentum* and *velocity.* When contemplating large-scale changes, the enormity of the task may seem overwhelming and even paralyzing. You may see what you want with crystal clarity and have the skills to achieve your dream. Indeed, you may also have an extensive support team of family, friends, and experts. Still, the sheer size of the task could keep you from taking even the first simple step. (However, you'll overcome this inertia by following the six steps in *The System.)*

5. *I assume you have the ability to take effective action.* The straightforward ideas presented in this system don't work for everyone or match every situation you face. If the action ideas aren't for you, follow the advice in Chapter Five and seek other resources. If you have special needs or challenges, it may be appropriate to seek professional assistance. Remember, where there's a will, there's always a way.

6. *I assume you're open to changing your behavior if necessary.* Doing what you did *yesterday* won't be enough to move you toward achieving your personal and professional goals *today*. A shift in results inherently requires a change in behavior. For many people, incremental daily changes do the trick. For others, scrapping old habits and belief systems might be in order. If you're open to change now, let's go!

MY QUALIFICATIONS AND APPROACH

What qualifies me to offer this *Do What You Can System* for changing your life? Am I a therapist, life coach, counselor, social worker, prophet, or some sort of wizard? No, none of these. I'm a Certified Public Accountant and consultant—a fact-based businessman. Observing how people behave is essential in my work. For thirty-five years, I've watched, asked, analyzed, assessed, concluded, and recommended. I've observed hundreds of people succeed in achieving their goals and just as many fail. In both my professional and personal life, I've repeatedly seen conduct that's led to positive results as well as behavior that's ended in frustration and disappointment.

Consider the following examples of effective actions that successful, purposeful people take every day.

- *To improve the quality of your relationships, show people they're important through your words and tone and through your daily interactions with them.*

- *To advance your career, do the best job you can every day while making others aware of your value to the organization.*

- *To get a new job, present yourself well, communicate the benefits you bring to the employer, and articulate exactly why it would be in the organization's best interests to hire you.*

- *To manage your weight and health, control the quality and quantity of what you eat and how you burn those calories.*

- *To build a financial safety net, develop financial literacy, save consistently, and manage your financial risks.*

These effective actions are simple in concept, but can be challenging to sustain. Likewise, the six-step *Do What You Can System* is simple in concept but will take conscious effort to implement and sustain in your life. Why? Because it requires you to replace results-limiting habits with solutions-focused actions based on *your* definition of better choices for your life.

Are you curious to know the actions that have worked for others as well as those that have blocked their success? I've based my *Do What You Can System* on six action steps that, as I've observed, mean the difference between disappointment and success. I've applied *The System* effectively in my own life and I'm confident it will work for you too—*if* you follow it, take action, and stay committed to your goals.

WHAT TO EXPECT FROM *THE SYSTEM*

By working through what *The System* demands, you can expect to feel empowered to make the changes you want, with the resources you have, for whatever situation you find yourself in today.

Chapter One helps you analyze where you came from—your family, education, relationships, and career. You'll identify strengths you have to aid in initiating the changes you wish to make. You'll recognize skills and knowledge that perhaps you didn't realize you had. In Step 1, you'll also identify ineffective behaviors and habits you've accumulated. In business terms, Step 1 examines your current state of strengths, weaknesses, opportunities, and threats.

In Chapter Two, you'll answer the questions "What's next? What do I really want? And why do I want it?" Step 2 requires you to brainstorm the changes you want to make and define your far-horizon goals. After identifying the reasons behind why these goals are important to you, you'll record the results of this brainstorming, listing your intended changes in general terms.

Chapter Three guides you to visualize your goals and objectives. In Step 3, you'll detail your goals from Step 2, using all five senses to paint a vivid picture of what your world will look like once you've achieved them. Doing this provides the necessary framework for action.

Doing these first three steps well is absolutely critical to your success. Resist the temptation to skip over them and move quickly to action. As Henry Ford said, "Thinking is the hardest work there is, which is probably the reason why so few engage in it." Take the time to be abundantly clear about what you want to accomplish before creating your action plan. Concentrate first on the *what, where,* and *why* of your goals. Only after they're complete do you move on to your *how.*

Chapter Four addresses the *how* part of the *Do What You Can System.* In Step 4, you'll develop short- and long-term action plans for each goal you specified in Step 2 and further described in Step 3. You'll also draw on the skills and abilities you listed in Step 1 as you create your solutions-focused plan.

Chapter Five (Step 5) gets you to jump into action. All of your brainstorming, visualizing, and planning will be put to the test of discipline. Because change demands sustained daily behavior, this is when the real fun begins—when you can see the early fruits of your efforts.

As you put your Step 5 plans into effect, Chapter Six shows you how to measure and track your results. It coaches you to consider the evolving world around you and modify your approach accordingly without losing sight of your goals.

Chapter Seven will be a surprise. Rest assured, by staying fully engaged in *The System* through Chapter Six, it will help you appreciate the true potential of these ideas as they catch on. Imagine what might happen when thousands of people clarify and pursue their life dreams!

Chapter Eight provides a quick-reference summary of all six steps. Once you're immersed in fine-tuning your plans with daily action, it will help you stay on track and reinforce the big picture you're painting.

PURPOSE, BALANCE, AND VALUES

What's your ultimate goal in working through *The System*?

To identify your purpose in this world at this time and then take effective action to support it.

A sound idea in theory. However, the practical challenge comes when working with the real-world limitations of information, ability, and time. So as you pursue your goals, be sure to embrace the powerful concept of balance. Find the right balance between goals and limitations—a simple concept but not always easy.

No matter what the challenges, I remind you to pursue your goals with energy, passion, playfulness, and great joy. What's the point if going through the six steps doesn't bring you fun and satisfaction? Make it a joyful part of your life.

As you work through the six steps, keep these values in mind:

- *Commit to the core themes of personal responsibility, usable ideas, systematic process, and effective action to achieve the changes you want.*

- *Fully accept who you are and where you are in your life.*

- *Be 100 percent responsible for where you want to go and how you'll get there.*

- *Have the confidence to face doubt and fear and to counteract their influence.*

- *For the greatest return on your investment, make service to others a fundamental operating principle of your life.*

Remember, to get large-scale results that differ from what you're currently experiencing requires acting differently. It also requires assessing your resistance to change, knowing it directly affects your likelihood of success.

LIVE WITH A SENSE OF EXCITEMENT

I'm excited about *The System* and its benefits for you. I challenge you to seek that same excitement and sense of purpose, too. Bring it into every aspect of your life—at work, at home, everywhere.

I further challenge you to actively change those aspects of your life that don't excite you. Energize yourself and each person you touch—not through artificial feel-good cheerleading but through living every day completely aligned with your fundamental life purpose. If you can do this, you'll experience an abundance of success, fun, energy, and peace of mind well beyond your imagination.

You'll be amazed at how your success expands when you have the support and structure to grow your possibilities. Learn from my parents' example: Decide what's important. Know what you want to accomplish. Then get up every day and do what needs to be done.

Get ready to break the boundaries of your past and grow confidently to your future. Let's get started.

STOP, LOOK, AND LISTEN

Life's major transition points are intersections that focus your awareness on where you are. Your options are open—you can make a conscious decision to continue as before, turn in a new direction, or come to a stop.

Transition points also focus your attention on where you've been—all the life tools, skills, and habits you've accumulated along the way. Consider them major meeting points of the past, present, and future.

WHAT MAJOR INTERSECTIONS LOOK LIKE

Some life intersections gradually grow from a passing thought into an obsession you can't ignore. Other intersections are thrust on you without warning. Let's look at a few real-life examples.

BECKY

Becky is a forty-four-year-old mother of two boys, ages 17 and 15. Becky and her husband, Jack, work long hours to meet the family's expenses and provide a private school education for their sons. Their four-bedroom home is located on a half-acre lot on a quiet street in a safe city neighborhood.

Happily married, Becky and Jack strive to balance the responsibilities that come with being good parents, owning a home, advancing their careers, and providing each other with opportunities to grow, both together and as individuals. As their boys become more independent, Becky feels a mixture of happiness at their growth and uncertainty about what her role will be once they're off to college. With family responsibilities shrinking, she seeks greater fulfillment in her job as a project manager for a software company. But lately, the job feels routine, even boring. She can do it without even thinking.

Naturally, Becky wonders, "What's next?"

With the boys out of the house most evenings, Becky and Jack enjoy quiet time together. But is their life becoming *too* quiet? Although Becky's happy, she's also restless. Sitting outside in the sun one Saturday afternoon, she lists her interests and skills on a piece of paper and then asks, "What do I need to learn to grow into the next phase of my life?"

MIKE

Mike willingly supports thirty-five sales representatives, answering their questions daily by email and phone. He enters customer orders into the company's computer system and has developed a reputation for accuracy and quality. Mike's supervisors recognize his importance to the organization and, through the company's annual performance review process, make sure he receives maximum rewards. Aware that his bosses take good care of him, Mike does his best in return. Yet in recent months, he feels a growing sense of restlessness and doubt. His mind keeps returning to the same question about his job: "Is this all there is?"

At least today, the routine changed. Mike's counterpart, Sue, is visiting from another office. Over lunch, they compare notes about their common job responsibilities and gossip a bit. With no prompting on Mike's part, Sue mentions her concerns about their future prospects at the company. Both Mike and Sue are needed by the departments they support. However, this makes Sue worry that she might not be considered seriously for advancement because her absence would leave a vacuum. In a moment of clarity, Mike realizes he feels the same way.

Back at his desk that afternoon, Mike reflects on his work, his family, and his relationship with his parents. He also ponders the status of his spirit. He isn't sad or melancholy, just more aware—more in the present. The conversation with Sue has pulled these thoughts from the dark corners of his mind to a front-and-center position.

On his drive home that evening, Mike enjoys the warm spring breeze through the open car window and listens to a favorite song on the radio. Close to home, the road crosses railroad tracks. As he does every evening, Mike turns down the music and brakes as he approaches the crossing, bringing the car to a full stop. He looks left and right down the tracks and listens carefully. For a few important seconds, he concentrates completely, blocking out all other thoughts. When he's sure no train is coming, he proceeds carefully across the tracks and continues home.

As he drives on, Mike realizes his conscious actions at this intersection of road and rail are wise—the result of a life lesson. Similarly, at life's major intersections where past, present, and future meet, it's wise to stop and take notice. To concentrate and look around. To listen.

At home that night, Mike lists possible jobs he might pursue next in his career. He also lists the skills he has now and those he might need for that next job.

ANDREA

Andrea has mixed feelings about her job. On one hand, she feels fortunate to have survived three rounds of layoffs at her company in the last two years. But as a survivor, she's been forced to assume the work of two people—her former coworker's job and her own. So her days are long, and she finishes every week too exhausted to fully enjoy the weekend. With the economy in terrible shape, she's not sure what to do about her situation, but she knows she has to do something. She just can't sustain her current exhausting path.

DAVID

Now thirty-two, David has served his country as a soldier since he was eighteen. Through that experience, he's matured, gained confidence, and grown into a dependable leader. His technical specialty in electronics and communications should help him secure a job in the civilian world, and his fluency in three languages should interest employers with operations overseas.

With only three months left in his military commitment, David decides it's time to get serious about life after the Army. After all, for nearly fifteen years, his military responsibilities have ruled his decisions.

Early one morning, David takes a pad of paper and a pen and finds a quiet place to sit and think. He makes two lists: One highlights his strengths and abilities; the other details the challenges he must overcome to build a life in the civilian world. With plenty of possibilities laid out before him, he finds the exercise exciting—but also intimidating. Large-scale life transitions are just that.

SALLY

Sally enjoyed her six-week trip that's ending in a few days. Throughout her career, she had never taken that much time away. However, now that she's been retired for almost a year, she can just about go anywhere and do anything for as long as she wants. That's why she worked hard all those years.

So what's the problem? A little voice in Sally's head seems to think a problem is lurking. It speaks up several times a day, getting her attention like a tap on the shoulder. Sally still has many years ahead of her to be productive. "What are you going to do now that's important?" the little voice keeps asking.

ROGER

Roger looks up at the ambulance attendant hovering over him. He tastes the dry oxygen flowing in through the mask on his face and feels a heavy pressure in his chest. He hears the wail of the siren over the beep-beep-beep of the heart monitor as the ambulance weaves through traffic on the way to the emergency room. Being strapped down on his back feels strange to Roger. He's afraid of what's to come. He's also aware he feels disappointed in his body that is failing him.

All those years of no exercise, carrying an extra forty pounds, and eating and drinking whatever he wanted, his body never even gave him a hint that anything might be wrong—until now. Yet the message is coming through loud and clear on this day. Even as the ambulance backs up to the hospital doors, Roger makes a mental checklist of the changes he'll make in his life as soon as he's back on his feet.

STEP 1: AWARENESS OF WHAT IS NOW

Step 1 of the *Do What You Can System* involves acknowledging that every day, our past and future intersect. Absent a specific reason to pay attention, many of us fail to even notice. For Becky, awareness of her family and career intersection happened gradually as her boys became more self-sufficient. For Mike, a visit from a coworker brought subconscious doubts about his advancement to the surface. Andrea's exhaustion is forcing her to make tough decisions about her job. David's imminent release from military service is urging him to prepare for what comes next. Sally needed a year of retirement to bring out her little voice. A medical emergency forced Roger to take a hard look at his unhealthy habits and pledge to pursue wellness and health.

Different situations, one common experience: *They were all prompted to examine where they were, where they wanted to go, and what skills and habits they would need to move in new directions.*

Like Becky, Mike, and Andrea, you might feel a desire to change after a period of increasing awareness. Sally and David became well aware of major life changes that came from ending long-term employment and starting in a radically new direction. Unfortunately, like Roger, you might be shocked into change by a life-challenging train roaring down the tracks.

Step 1 requires you to interrupt the buzz of your life and just stop, look, and listen. Set aside time to examine your relevant history and your current abilities and life skills honestly and objectively. This step requires you to consciously examine your starting point for change—*where you came from*—and then, in Roosevelt's terms, deeply examine *where you are* and *what you've got*.

You'll also examine both real and imagined barriers to growth and change in your life. You'll ferret out the bad habits, personal deceptions, and invalid excuses that hold you back. You'll identify the payoffs you think you'll receive from allowing them to exist.

By following the suggestions and exercises, you'll complete Step 1 with these assets:

- *A list of strengths and the life tools you brought with you from your past*
- *A conscious awareness of barriers*
- *A sharper focus on the direction you want to head*

Right now today, you've arrived at a life intersection. What a great time to stop, look, and listen!

WHERE YOU CAME FROM—YOUR FOUNDATION FOR GROWTH

Your foundation for growth consists of the solid facts from your past that you've built on as you've moved through your life. As you pursue your purpose and life goals from here on, you don't abandon your past—you *continue* to build on it. Always be aware of your foundation; when uncertainty creeps into your decisions, refer to these foundational blocks for reassurance.

You'll notice that some attributes of your foundation remain stable as you change, at least into the foreseeable future. For example, my current height is seventy-three inches. This fact is an attribute of my foundation, my physical world; I expect it will remain constant. Another fact is my age. Each year I remain alive, this number will go up; it can't go down or remain the same. Barring a major unforeseen event, I know what to expect of my height and age. Therefore, they can be relied upon when I visualize my desired results.

What other foundation factors are relevant to your goals? You'd include your governing beliefs, ethics and morals, communications skills, family and extended support systems, work and professional experience, and financial stability, to name a few. Your foundation also includes the filters through which you see the world—the ones that cover critical core growth issues. For example, are you inherently programmed for success, mediocrity, or failure? For calm or action? For peace or aggression? For helping or ignoring the needs of others? How have you been programmed by life to this point? Examine your programming filters—such influences as family, religion, friends, education, experiences, income, financial security, race, age, nationality, geography, occupation, and physical well-being.

Having conscious awareness of your life facts, existing skills, filters, and barriers is crucial in defining what you want to change and how you'll do so. "Where are you from?" is more than a polite question you ask when you meet someone for the first time. The full answer provides a frame of reference and crucial points of comparison to your own past.

What important attributes of your past relate to your willingness or unwillingness to act in a radically different manner (if that's what you need to achieve your goals)? What strengths do you bring? And what heavy anchors from your past continue to slow you down?

MY OWN ANALYSIS OF WHERE I'M FROM

Let me answer a few of these questions regarding my own past. I provide these details for two reasons: first, to give you an example of the type of analysis I'd like *you* to perform; second, to give you hints about my perspective on the *Do What You Can System*.

As of this writing in 2011, I'm fifty-five years old and happily married. My wife, Kris, and I have no children. We live in the mountains of Colorado in a five-year-old mid-sized home with an enormous mortgage.

I was born in Philadelphia, Pennsylvania, the fourth of five children. I'm the favorite, of course. My parents were married for over sixty-five years before my father passed away a year ago at age eighty-seven. My mother is now eighty-seven. My parents have been constant, positive figures throughout my life.

I attended large Catholic schools in Philadelphia for eight years of elementary school and four years of high school. During my school years, we lived in a row house. The corner house on our block, it was perhaps a few feet wider than the other houses on the street but still modest in size and amenities. Seven in the house. Four bedrooms. One bathroom. Do the math.

Our elementary school was only three city blocks away, but getting to high school involved a twenty-minute drive or, more often, an hour trip by foot, subway, and bus. With more than 6,000 students at the high school, having control and discipline were critical. Our dedicated teachers did the best they could to teach and lead us while maintaining that control and discipline.

Earning good grades after copious memorizing, I earned a college degree in accounting from Penn State University, a state school with huge classes and little individual attention. Fortunately, I was hired by an international accounting firm immediately after college and became a Certified Public Accountant. Five years later, I switched to a position in a large company and became one of about 90,000 employees. For the last twenty years, I've been a self-employed public speaker, trainer, and consultant.

When it comes to beliefs, I'm a highly spiritual person who believes in God and the existence of an afterlife. My politics are fact-based and I have minimal tolerance for mediocrity. I especially dislike untruths (more commonly known as lies) that are spouted by too many politicians and "talking heads" in the media.

My relevant skill set includes an ability and willingness to speak to audiences on business, self-management, and personal improvement. I'm logical, and I follow the rules (just as I've been taught). I possess a solid working knowledge of the business skills of accounting, cash modeling, short- and long-range planning, risk awareness and remediation, and communications. I'm good at what I do, but many others are better—and I want to continue learning from them all.

This snapshot of "where I'm from" naturally remains a large part of who and what I am today. I simply can't ignore how I was taught to think and act. Conformity dominated my religion, my schooling, and the first half of my professional career. Both in school and at work, advancement and recognition came as much from slogging it out over time as from technique, subtlety, and application of skills. My parents and teachers taught me to keep my head down and keep working. "Don't talk back and don't ask questions."

This makes up my personal programming—where I'm from and how I was raised (school, church, neighborhood, work experience, friends, and relatives). My foundation includes these attributes:

- *Reliable, loving parents and a secure home and family environment*

- *Discipline to follow rules or face certain consequences*

- *Pattern of blending in with the crowd, including not thinking for myself, not sticking out in any way, and not exploring what I could be*

- *Tendency to be pulled by good luck and circumstances rather than deliberately striking out from the pack*

- *History of taking instruction from safe traditional sources of authority—parents, family, teachers, church, supervisors*
- *Sustained habit of working hard*
- *Character of reliability*
- *Ability to think analytically and logically*

In short, point me in the right direction and I'd go there!

This foundation has served me well and continues to be the base on which I build each day. However, as a result of challenges I experienced fifteen years into my career, one day—like Mike did in the earlier scenario—I asked myself, "Is this all there is?" A decision point, an intersection, came into my awareness. A time to stop, look, and listen—to decide if this was the path I wanted to sustain.

After several months of pausing, assessing, and allowing my thoughts to wander to various possibilities, I decided to move in new directions. That transition has reached its twentieth year—and it's still a work in process!

Yes, I built on several foundational attributes noted—reliability, hard work, analysis, and logic. More important, I left behind filters and behaviors that became barriers to what I perceived as my core life purpose. These barriers included

- *Seeking approval from others;*
- *Being content to blend in when I really wanted to chart my own path;*
- *Being tied to a full time commitment working in large business organizations;*
- *Accepting as fact statements made by politicians, media personalities, and official spokespeople; and*

- *Blindly following rules made by authority figures. (Instead, I must understand why a rule exists and decide if it makes sense to follow. If it doesn't make sense, I put it aside and accept the consequences of not following it.)*

EXERCISE: WHAT'S YOUR STORY?

Complete the following exercise. You'll have the best results if you find a quiet place to write without distractions or interruptions. Don't skip any part of it; work through all three parts. Record your answers using a computer, a pen, a crayon—whatever works for you—and write down your answers *in detail.*

I suggest you allot a minimum of an hour to do this exercise. However, you may want to allow a few days for reflection. Simply give yourself the gift of quiet and the time it naturally takes to complete it. It will help you become more aware of the "where you are" and "what you've got" that Teddy Roosevelt talked about.

Part One

In your thoughts, go back in time and walk through the major stages of your life:

- *Your preschool, primary and secondary education*
- *Your advanced education if you have it*
- *Your teen, young adult, and later years*
- *Your various jobs and career positions*
- *Your married (or otherwise committed) life*
- *Your child or children (if applicable)*

Be complete. List as many of these life periods or experience categories as you can recall. Additional categories might be My Current Job, My College Years, or My Military Service. Aim for five to ten separate categories, depending on your age and the diversity of your life experiences.

As you write, leave room between each category for notes, or use a fresh page for each one.

Part Two

Once you've listed your categories, reflect on and complete notes about each one before moving to the next. Record the skills, abilities, strengths, and other positive foundational attributes you attained in each category. Your list might read something like this:

- *When I was a child, from my parents I learned respect, reliability, and honesty.*

- *In my job with a newspaper during the '90s, I learned how to write effectively.*

- *During my military service, I learned leadership skills.*

- *From my current job in which I supervise a team of five, I learned how to mentor and coach others and evaluate their business performance.*

- *Working in my community or church group, I learned compassion.*

- *As a parent and in my marriage, I learned understanding, patience, and tolerance.*

When you've finished, go back through your list and identify your most important skills, abilities, strengths, and other positive attributes. From these, select and write down on a separate sheet the top ten positive attributes you'll use as you implement the changes you want to make.

Part Three

As you did for Part Two, reflect on each life category from Part One, completing each category before moving on to the next. But this time, record any habits, excuses, or other barriers to growth that you still have that you know are holding you back from achieving your purpose. It might include

- *Being satisfied with doing an adequate job when you know you could do much better,*
- *Not taking time to tell those important to you how much you appreciate them,*
- *Not eating healthy,*
- *Not getting enough sleep,*
- *Not thinking for yourself,*
- *Mindlessly watching far too much television,*
- *Avoiding new people and unfamiliar experiences,*
- *Letting too many of your actions be driven by what others say you should do rather than what **you know** you should do.*

When you're finished, go back through the results and identify the ten most significant habits, beliefs, or excuses you choose to leave behind. On a separate sheet, write down what you'll do instead. For example, you'd say, "I will do what I know I should do rather than react to the wishes of others. I will learn about nutrition and eat food that's good for me. I will turn off the TV and go for a long walk. I will seek the truth in statements by authority figures rather than accept what I hear."

Congratulations! In completing this exercise, you stopped, you looked, and you listened. You decided what to take with you from your past and what to leave behind. As a result, you're well on the way to creating a compelling vision of what *you* want to accomplish.

Take a moment to smile. You earned it.

WHY PEOPLE RESIST POSITIVE CHANGE

In the exercise you just completed, you identified excuses and habits that hold you back. In this section, I describe the five most common excuses for avoiding growth that I've observed.

I've been an auditor for thirty-five years and I realize the term *auditor* means many things to many people. Images of an inflexible, humorless tax auditor may come to mind or even a long-suffering corporate drone who tracks innumerable, lifeless accounting details.

Let me set the record straight—you're an auditor, too. To audit is to review. On a Saturday evening in a neighborhood restaurant, you audit the charges on your dinner check before paying the bill. Each month, you audit the details of your credit card statements and bank account summaries to make sure that only authorized activity is included. In these activities, everyone is an auditor to one degree or another, which may come as a surprise to any amateur auditors in training.

As a *professional* auditor, my role is different. Yes, a lot of business fact checking forms the basis of the work, but it goes much further. My work includes looking at individual, work group, and process performances that fall short of their targets. I quantify the gap between leader expectations or established standards and the actual results obtained. That part of auditing is considered routine for someone with my background and years of experience.

However, the most important—and often most difficult—step in business auditing involves identifying the core reasons *why* performance results fall below standards. The difficulty is compounded when I'm asked to motivate the humans in the equation to change their behavior and meet the standards set by senior management. More often than not, my suggestions on how to resolve the business issue are met with strong resistance—even when the changed behavior would solve the problem, reward those who make the change, and make their work lives easier to manage. This has led me to wonder "Do adult humans naturally resist change?"

After years of observing, I believe that, in general, people don't resist changes filled with opportunities to move toward what we want. For example, we get married, start families, send our children off to school, change jobs, or move to a different city without undue resistance because we chose to do so. But people do tend to resist change that's forced on them, so they mask that resistance with one or more excuses.

The following are five of my favorite excuses.

Excuse 1: *"That's the way I've always done it."*

"I'm more comfortable with the way I've always done it."

"What if my boss/subordinates/associates consider my use of your idea a sign of weakness?"

"What if I'm just not as good at my job if I try the new method?"

I've heard fear-based reasons like these too many times to count. I understand that doing things differently from the norm can cause feelings of uncertainty, anxiety, or even tension. After all, it's new! But is it the type of fear that should paralyze adults and keep them from trying something different?

Some people use fear of change as an excuse to avoid trying, saying, "What if it doesn't work? I'll look silly for trying." Remember what I do as an auditor? I look hard at individuals, processes, and teams that fail to meet expectations. Based on that, I conclude that fighting to do the same thing they've always done will most certainly look silly if leaders are already disappointed with their performance. In the same manner, if you're disappointed with the results you achieve in your personal life, fighting with yourself to *continue* to do what you've always done simply doesn't make sense.

In your head and your heart, you know that improvement requires change. Moving from disappointing results to meeting your performance targets requires doing something different—like changing your programming from "I'm afraid I'll look silly" to "I want to look like someone who's interested in improvement."

Excuse 2: "The benefits don't exceed the costs."

People love to use this excuse in the business world. It gives the appearance that someone performed a sound, reasoned, dispassionate calculation of the benefits expected compared to the calculated cost of making the change. Unfortunately, in business as in life, dispassionate analysis rarely takes place.

As an auditor wanting to influence individual or organizational behavior, when I hear this excuse, I ask this question: "Did you actually perform a detailed review of the benefits and costs? If so, please show it to me." On occasion, I'm given a well-researched, rational analysis of the benefits and costs of the potential change. However, in my thirty-five years of work experience, I'm confident I can count those occasions on the fingers of both hands with a few fingers left over.

To counteract this excuse for avoiding change, it may help to minimize the risk by breaking the new behavior into small steps. Pick one small step and try it. Focus on the benefits. And be definite about the changes you'll make in your behavior. Here are a few examples of the steps you might take:

- *Want to get in shape? Start by walking around the block each day, then walk a little farther each time you set out.*

- *Want to get a better performance rating in your job? Offer one improvement idea in your next conversation with your supervisor. Then repeat this every few days or every week until your supervisor regards you as someone who's interested in improvement.*

- *Want to improve the quality of your marriage or your relationship with your children? Today, say something nice to your spouse or your challenging child. Do it again tomorrow and every day at least once a day. Do it with certainty. If you focus even for just a few seconds, you'll quickly notice opportunities to say something nice.*

Start with small changes that feel safe and look for evidence that your modest behavior efforts have paid off. Tackle big issues over time as you get more comfortable with these new behaviors.

Excuse 3: "I'm not clear on what I want to do."

Lack of clarity about your desired results poses problems. "I wish I weighed less" versus "I'm going to lose fifteen pounds in the next three months" convey two different statements. The first lacks precision; the second contains a specific, measurable goal and a time deadline for results. The first statement is a wish; the second is a command. Which has a greater chance of success? In their thought-provoking book *Switch,* authors Chip and Dan Heath remind us of the importance of a clear destination when they say, "Some is not a number; soon is not a time."[1]

Humans are inherently visual creatures (a theme you'll see in Step 3, Chapter Three). Creating and communicating a detailed description of what will happen—and what it will look like—is important to affect individual and group change. In business, leaders need to address this barrier by creating a clear, compelling picture of what the change will *look* like when it's completed. It must include a description of the role each person plays and how progress will be measured.

To change your own behavior requires having a clear image of what your new behavior will look like, what steps you'll take, and how you'll measure your progress.

Each of these large-scale change-management stages—describing a clear picture of the result, creating a written plan of the steps you'll take, and determining how improvement will be measured—are covered in later chapters.

Excuse 4: "I don't know how to do that!"

It would be unwise to take up skydiving as a hobby without taking a few lessons first. Likewise, it's unfair to expect employees and work teams to perform tasks in a new way but fail to teach them how to do so.

Time after time, I've witnessed new policies and directives issued from an organization's headquarters without the skills training needed to implement the new procedures properly. When that happens, well-meaning employees do their best based on their interpretation of what they think is required. The result? Lack of consistency, confusion, and results that fail to meet expectations.

In a similar manner, as you pursue your own goals, lacking certain skills can block your progress. Are you unhappy with the quality of your relationship with your children, spouse, or business associates? Are you unable to communicate effectively with people who are important to you? Do you consistently fail to get the physical conditioning results you imagined? The cause of any of these could be a legitimate lack of skills, which you can resolve (as you'll see in Step 4, Chapter Four).

Excuse 5: "I just don't want to!"

Children freely and honestly express resistance to their parents. "I don't want to!" is the refrain of toddlers learning about free will and resisting their parents' instructions. "Put away your toys." "Eat your vegetables." "Stop kicking the seat of the nice airline passenger sitting in front of you." (I couldn't resist throwing that one in!) The child's response of "I don't want to!" puts the parent in the position of forcefully intervening.

Of course, few adults admit *this* excuse for resisting change. They don't want to risk sounding like a toddler! Instead, "I don't want to" gets masked by other excuses, including those previously mentioned. But the core reason remains the same: "I can make up my own mind, and I've decided I don't want to do what you're suggesting." You've heard them: "I don't want to go to the gym; I don't want to stop eating junk food; I don't want to follow the new directive from headquarters." At least these responses are honest.

I believe most people want to move toward a life aligned with their purpose, dreams, expectations, and desires. But let me be especially clear. If you're resisting and simply "don't want to" search your soul and make the changes needed to align your results with your desires, expectations, and goals, *that's okay.* If you're happy with what is and where you are, *that's okay, too.*

The objective is to bring any limiting excuses, behaviors, and habits to the conscious level. There, you can examine them and see if you want to stay on your current course—or change. Again, either way is okay. Successful people often decide not to take action based on their analysis rather than their lack of will or other excuses.

The bottom line? Be honest with yourself. Examine every excuse you use and decide once and for all to leave behind all that hold you back.

TRUTH, LIES, AND PAYOFFS

Not only excuses but all forms of untruth can weigh you down and hold you back.

Most people claim to seek truth and tell the truth. They dislike being deceived and maintain a low opinion of anyone who tries to con them. Once they're aware they've been targeted for deception, they avoid trusting the offending party again.

Yet every day, we can deceive *ourselves.* We may say we're taking care of our bodies but make poor choices in the food and drinks we consume. We may convince ourselves we're saving enough money for emergencies or retirement when we know we're just one unfortunate event away from financial crisis. We may repeatedly ignore posted speed limits and litter the streets with cigarette butts and trash while maintaining the fiction that we're law-abiding citizens. We may still start each day with a long list of what we'll accomplish, even though our record of devoting energy to busywork is clear, so we procrastinate.

We also say we want the truth from others—but do we *really* want to know? We tell our teenage children we want them to talk to us about anything and report what happens when they're out with friends. We proclaim that we want our bosses to tell us how we're doing. And when we give ourselves feedback, we believe we can objectively evaluate our own performances. In the political arena, we say we want honest politicians who are interested in doing "the people's work" objectively.

But what's the reality? Despite all our beliefs to the contrary, we have difficulty with absolute truth. We resist receiving honest, objective feedback from others and favorably shade the feedback we give ourselves, claiming the benefit of the doubt when the facts don't meet our expectations. We want to believe our teenage children are perfect when they're not under our direct observation—and that's how we ignore what *we* did at their age! We don't heed speed limits because "no one else does" and "it's not really wrong" to exceed them. We vote for politicians who make promises we want to hear, even when we know those promises ignore the reality of limited budgets and other critical resources.

Winston Churchill may have said it best. "Men occasionally stumble over the truth, but most pick themselves up and hurry off as if nothing has happened."

Like the people in the following examples, most people cover up, justify, and stall.

BOBBY

Bobby's kids don't listen when he speaks to them calmly and rationally, so he yells and threatens them. He knows this approach doesn't constitute good parenting, but he justifies his behavior with the belief that it isn't doing any long-term harm to the kids. He simply doesn't want to face the fact that his behavior is abusive.

TERI

Teri stands outside her office building in the rain to smoke. Recently, she read an article about reducing the number of cigarettes smoked each day as being positive change. She interpreted this information to mean that her half-dozen smoking breaks every day are much healthier than the dozen or more she took just a few months ago. She can't face the truth that she's slowly poisoning herself *every time* she lights up.

MICHAEL

Michael tells his wife he's having dinner with a client when he's actually heading out to a bar with male and female coworkers for a few drinks and dancing. He tells himself he's entitled to blow off steam after work every now and then. And if he told his wife that, she'd only worry for no reason.

WHY DO YOU NEED TRUTH?

Why do so many people behave this way? Why do we allow the paradox of detesting deception by others while condoning it in ourselves? Why do we both preach and resist truth? What are the payoffs? Certainly not to gain accurate information for making informed decisions, building relationships, or assessing life's risks. Quite the opposite.

We allow ourselves to continue to act in ways that we know hold back our growth or cause harm. We take the easy way out when making a change is crucial. We avoid the work and uncertainty that pursuing our goals requires. All the while, we rationalize our improper behavior. As a result, we end up with flawed information, faulty decisions, and poor results. That's the payoff, and that's the truth.

Having sources where you find absolute truth is critical to your ability to think realistically, evaluate options and capabilities, make accurate decisions about what you can accomplish, and create an action plan for positive change. How honest are you about yourself? What are your most reliable sources of honest feedback?

Yes, truth is necessary to make sound decisions, grow in a healthy, sustainable manner, manage risks and barriers to success, and achieve your goals. This applies to business, government, education, organized religion, and most certainly in your personal life.

Can you pinpoint your sources of truth in your marriage, family, work, health, and personal results measurements? Do you realize that continuing to deceive yourself and striving to achieve your goals inherently contradict each other?

Do your best to have truth in your thinking, your skills, your data, and the measurements of your results. Find and face truth. Give honest but empathetic feedback to others. Eliminate the lies you tell yourself along with the payoffs you believe you get from deception.

Be truth.

ELIMINATING BARRIERS

Barriers prevent progress and separate you from what you want. They take the form of the people, habits, organizations, flawed beliefs, and limited resources that keep you from achieving your goals. Some days, they fill your time and totally get in your way.

The barriers you deal with can be real, legitimate, and unavoidable. If you want to perform surgery, lack of medical training, field experience, and a license to practice hold you back. For me to play professional basketball, legitimate barriers include my age, lack of speed, and new double knee replacements. And don't even get me started on my inability to dribble a basketball with my left hand!

These kinds of barriers to transformation require conscious management of real-world realities, addressed in Chapter Six. Other barriers mentioned earlier include avoiding truth, accepting deception, and making excuses for not changing behavior.

Yet some barriers *can* be managed easily, so let's address them without delay. What minor changes can you make to actions you already take each day? Consider the following eight thought barriers as a way to take Roosevelt's advice and act where you are with what you've got.

Barrier 1: "Other people are responsible for my results."

Guess what. They aren't. *You* are. Others may have legitimate power over you in certain situations: supervisors at work, security personnel at airports, teachers and administrators at school, parents over children. In the short run, others may dictate your behavior and influence the results. But in the long run, embrace the fact that you *alone* are responsible for your results. It's true. Get used to it.

Barrier 2: "I give in to distractions."

While driving in the mountains last spring, I paid attention as a car sped past me. I saw the driver talking on a mobile phone cradled between his right ear and his shoulder while texting (or something similar) on a second device with his left hand. This was nine o'clock Easter Sunday morning. And it was snowing!

Sure, certain distractions can be welcome. It's important to decompress and recharge frequently. But pick the right time and place to be either focused or distracted. Be aware of the difference. Apply the habit of focus and be present where you are.

Barrier 3: "I let my thinking become lazy."

If the job you're doing requires brainstorming alternative solutions, give it your full attention. If you want to make changes in your life, concentrate on clearly defining those changes. Be specific about the resources you will need and the actions you must take. Then stay focused until you've made the adjustments you desire.

Barrier 4: "I get addicted to busy work."

Successful people have lists of what they believe they must do to accomplish their goals. "Busy work" rarely makes their lists. The inevitable paperwork and administrative tasks must be addressed, of course, but how tempting it is to use busy work as an excuse to avoid what really needs to be done.

The cure for this addiction? Plan your time well, then devote your most productive hours to those tasks that will move you toward your biggest goals.

Barrier 5: "I often accept poor quality."

After a wonderful dinner at a Chicago restaurant, my friend and I discussed the outstanding service from our waiter. As my friend commented, "These days, we're surprised by good service." In business, leaders often think the cost of quality too high and the incremental benefits too low to make the extra effort to achieve quality at a high level. As a result, *quality never improves.*

The solution? Refuse to accept poor quality, especially in the human aspects of customer service. Speak up and request what you're entitled to receive. More important, refuse to accept poor quality in your own efforts. Give your best. Others are entitled to it, and so are you!

Barrier 6: "I doubt I can do that."

Self-doubt limits your self-image and a poor self-image limits your potential. "I doubt I can do that" becomes an excuse for not trying. "I've never done that before" becomes a reason for never doing it in the future.

Remember, self-doubt and self-image are all in your mind. Replace your thoughts of doubt with this kind of attitude: "I've never done that before, but I'll give it a try." Soon you'll smile and say, "I didn't know I could do that. I wonder what else I can do I didn't know I could!"

Barrier 7: "I'm the center of the universe."

Do you know someone who believes that the world revolves around them? Perhaps a neighbor, coworker, relative, or friend? This is the person who acts as though only he or she matters—the one who relates every experience to the impact it has on his or her life. People like this will wear you down and suck the life right out of you—if you let them.

Yes, everyone is important, but no one person is more important than any other. Be aware of and respectful to every person in your life. Check your ego and never let it dominate situations.

Barrier 8: "I constantly seek the approval of others."

Don't buy into that! Strike a healthy balance between seeking your own approval for your actions and being mindful of the legitimate reactions of others. Getting approval from others as your prime motivator will always get in your way!

Says philosopher and author Dr. Wayne W. Dyer, "When approval seeking is a need, the possibilities for truth are all but wiped out."[2] Be mindful of over-relying on others' approval or disapproval when choosing a course of action. When and where appropriate seek input from those you respect, but rely on your own balanced internal feedback system for approval.

CHAPTER ONE

Chapter One asked: "Where exactly are you from and how did you get to where you are?" It started with these six scenarios about people who became aware of major intersections in their lives:

- *Becky's thoughts about what might come next in her life*

- *Mike's ride home after an eye-opening discussion with a coworker*

- *Andrea's inability to meet the demands of her job without putting her health at risk*

- *David's concerns about returning to civilian life*

- *Sally's nagging thoughts about what's really important*

- *Roger's unplanned trip to the hospital*

All these people faced good reasons to stop, look, and listen to where they were and how they got to that place. Perhaps you're now at a good intersection to stop and contemplate.

Step 1 of the *Do What You Can System* requires taking a few hours or even weeks to examine your strengths and weaknesses. In Roosevelt's terms, the exercises in Step 1 ask you to identify what you've got and where you are.

Step 1 also suggests developing a higher level of awareness of routine daily habits, asking, "Do these habits help or hinder where I want to go and who I want to be?" Keep a notebook with you. Record specific actions you take on a regular basis. Do you want to continue making the same choices or modify what you do for a different result? Jot down your answers. Focus on the small choices that are easy to change in the short run. For example, be more aware of what you eat, how you talk to others, how much you walk or sit, how often and how fast you drive, how much time you spend watching television, and especially how you treat your loved ones. Make small choices and changes right now. No excuses.

It may take you a while to make big adjustments involving the work you do, where you live, your physical condition, your financial reserves, and lifestyle changes you want for the next five or ten years and beyond. It requires you to reprogram your thinking, revise deep-seated habits, and adjust your behaviors substantially.

Both small- and large-scale adjustments start with conscious awareness of the skills and behaviors you want to keep, the habits and excuses you want to change. Every day, practice the art of stopping and observing. Be open to adjusting your approach to life. Like cleaning computer files, trash those programs you no longer want. Get rid of those outdated habits, beliefs, and thought barriers that hold you back.

In this chapter, you stopped, looked back at your past, and listened. Now it's time to face forward. In Chapter Two, Step 2, you'll look toward where you want to go.

CHAPTER TWO: DEFINE YOUR FAR HORIZON

Thursday morning, 7:23 a.m. United Airlines flight 339 window seat, right side. From Seattle, we lift off to the south heading to Denver, making a slow left turn as we climb and break through the clouds. The plane levels off. Mt. Rainier and Mt. Saint Helens can be clearly seen on the horizon to the south, their peaks prominent above the clouds and snow-covered hills below. While these two monumental markers, lit by the morning sun, remain visible, the details of other landscape features blur in the distance.

Like my view from the airplane window, in Step 2 of the *Do What You Can System*, your focus will be on the far horizon. You'll define the "mountains" and other prominent features of where you want to go and what you want to accomplish. Later, in Chapter Three, Step 3, you'll add detail to the blurry parts of your view. But for now, relax and look off into the distance—perhaps five to ten years. And get ready to describe what you see.

WHAT CAN YOU BE?

Aside from my family members and my wife, Kris, the one person who's had a great influence on me is Dr. Wayne W. Dyer. Starting with his 1976 book, *Your Erroneous Zones*, through his 2011 offering, *Excuses Begone!* I've found practical advice in the challenging questions and insightful suggestions in Dyer's work. In *Excuses Begone!* he writes, "As Abraham Maslow once observed about self-actualizing people: *They must be what they can be.*"[1]

This statement hit me hard. Too many years I followed the rules and ideas that I didn't initiate, while deep inside I *knew* I should head in other directions. No more following the path laid out for me by others—unless it was the path I'd choose for my own reasons.

To be clear, I'm not endorsing a life of careless disregard of commitments made. Rather, I'm suggesting actively pursuing what you *could be*—perhaps what you were *intended to be*—while honoring your existing obligations. How did Roosevelt express it? Doing what you can with what you've got right where you are.

Take a moment to think about what you *can be* and contrast that with what you've *chosen to be* up until now. What *can* you be?

RELAX AND THINK

As part of Step 2, you'll write a general description of where you want to be when you've achieved your goals. While life growth and transformation are never-ending processes, for the sake of planning and measurement, you'll use a timeline of five years into the future, and you'll assume by then you've accomplished what you set out to do today. You'll describe what you've achieved with respect to your goals in five years' time. After all, it always helps to know your destination before setting out.

These seven suggestions will get you started:

1. Imagine you wake up one morning and everything is perfect. What do you see, smell, hear, and feel? Where are

you? Who is with you? What do you look like? What are you planning to do that day?

2. For now, put aside the "where you're from" notes from Step 1. They're not relevant to this exercise but will be useful in Steps 3 and 4 in the next two chapters.

3. In his book, *How Successful People Think*, John C. Maxwell suggests that successful people "fight the hectic pace of life that discourages intentional thinking."[2] Set aside sufficient time—three to four hours—to concentrate on the exercises that follow. Reward yourself with quiet and time away from any distractions.

4. Although formal meditation would be valuable in preparation, even a few minutes of quiet time alone before starting can help. Clear your thoughts, take a deep breath, and relax.

5. Allow yourself to dream—to use your imagination. Have fun describing your desired changes just the way you see them on the horizon. Give no thought about how you will get there, avoiding the practical details at this point. Just assume that what you want to accomplish will happen.

6. Release anything that others may say you "should" do and replace it with intentional thinking about what *you* want to accomplish. Yes, there may be comfort and security in staying hidden in the pack, but there's no inherent danger in *thinking* outside of the pack. Focus on your own goals, not those of others. Be true to yourself, setting aside thoughts of compromise.

7. Set your sights on excellence and greatness. Mediocre goals are unacceptable here!

STEP 2: DEFINE YOUR VALUES, DESCRIBE YOUR DESTINATIONS

What things in life are most important to you? The first of two exercises in Step 2 asks you to be highly focused and make conscious choices among alternatives I've listed. Your purpose is to provide a written backdrop of attributes against which you'll compare your goals.

I find doing Exercise One brings me back to my center—to my overriding values—and helps me focus my brainstorming for Exercise Two. Plus, the results guide me in making important decisions. I hope that's true for you, too.

Immediately after completing the first exercise, proceed to the second, allowing adequate time to complete both without interruption.

EXERCISE ONE

Listed here are pairings of words and ideas that have implied meanings opposing each other. As you consider each pairing, *select the one that best aligns with who and what you want in a perfect world.* Circle or check the word you want or write it on a separate sheet of paper. Ready? Let's go.

Life—Death

Health—Disease

Energized—Exhausted

Together/With—Against/Opposed

Trust—Distrust

Abundance—Scarcity

Growth—Stagnation/Decline

Happy—Sad

Peace—Violence

Satisfaction—Hunger

Faith—Doubt

Security—Fear

Clean—Polluted

Solutions—Problems

Responsibility—Neglect

Respect—Abuse

Honesty—Deceit

You probably selected the first word or idea in each pair, but perhaps not. The point is to be clear about your core values as you take a far-horizon view of your goals. And in case anything you deem important was absent in the word pairings above, add your own ideas to the list before moving on. For example, you might add "creative" or "strong" or other descriptive attributes that are vital to you.

Now take a few minutes and write down your results in sentence form on a separate sheet of paper. Here's an example:

I intend to have a healthy, energetic, abundant life. I want to interact at all times with people I trust and respect, who focus on solutions instead of problems, and are honest, responsible, and happy. Likewise, I want to offer these attributes—as well as honesty, peace, and security—to others through my own actions. I intend to always be responsible and honor my word.

Having such a clear statement of how you want to live your life supports you in making small- and large-scale decisions. Keep the results in front of you as you move to the next exercise and do other exercises in later chapters. Be consistent with the results you recorded and include the characteristics you identified in this first exercise.

EXERCISE TWO

In this second exercise, you'll work through seven areas of your life, ranging from the physical to the spiritual. While you'll address each area separately, keep in mind that all seven are interconnected and overlap significantly. Together, they constitute *your entire being*—which is important to remember as you proceed. (Don't worry. You'll be reminded again.)

Your assignment is to describe your far horizon, or destination, for each life area, and then describe yourself after you've made your desired changes.

All you need are a pad of paper, a pen or pencil, an open mind, and a comfortable place to work. If you invest a minimum of fifteen minutes on each of the seven areas, you'll finish in just under two hours—about the length of most movies.

Now relax, take a deep breath, and let your imagination run. Describe what you *really* want to see happen, including how you'll feel when you've accomplished your goals. Don't hold back.

In this imaginative space, focus on each of the following seven areas: The Physical You, The Interpersonal You, The Professional You, The Financial You, The Intellectual You, The Spiritual You, and The Psychological You.

1. **The Physical You.** This part of you involves the details of your daily physical existence. It includes your health and the condition of your body; where you live and work (home, office building, zoo, school, embassy, construction site, truck . . .); the type of weather where you live; and your surroundings. Think of macro details (what your general environment is like) and micro details (daily items such as the food you eat, the usual temperature, the look of your home inside and out, etc.).

    Your Assignment: Dream away! Resist the need to focus on *how* you will get from what *is* today to what

34

you *want* tomorrow. Be content to look out five years and describe what you see in your physical world after you've accomplished all your physical goals and created your perfect vision of your physical self and surroundings. What do you look like? What do you see when you look around you? Be sure to include how you *feel* about your physical existence.

You may find it helpful to refer to my vision as an example and fill in your own details.

The Physical Me

I'm now 60 years old, and I'm delighted to say I'm in excellent health. I'm the same weight I was five years ago, and I have more stamina and muscle strength. Each day, I eat in a healthy manner, focusing on the quality and source of what I consume.

My wife, Kris, and I work from our home in the Colorado mountains. In winter, we snowboard and snowshoe; in summer, we hike and bike. I enjoy reading every day. Together, Kris and I travel extensively for both business and personal reasons. We have friends both old and new in many locations.

My work involves giving presentations and workshops to large and small audiences. I also consult with organizations that have interesting purposes I want to support. I coach individuals dedicated to creating and attaining their goals and living their life's purpose.

---

2. **The Interpersonal You.** This area involves how you interact with other people once your goals have been accomplished and your transformation is complete. Do you

communicate clearly and effectively so others understand you? Are you an interested listener when others are talking? Can people rely on you without hesitation? Do you demonstrate an awareness of other people and show them courtesy and respect? Do you model positive behavior to your children, spouse or life partner, business associates, and strangers? When you slip up, do you take responsibility and corrective action? The new Interpersonal You includes all the key behavior and communications skills you'll have when you're fully transformed into the person you *can* be—complete with skills such as speaking, listening, writing, facilitating, and leading.

Your Assignment: Once more, look five years into the future when your life is better aligned with your purpose. Describe how you relate to others. List your interpersonal skills and how you use them. It may help to think of a few key relationships as you write down your answer. How would these important people describe The Interpersonal You at that time? (E.g., My boss (or spouse) says that I _____.)

3. **The Professional You.** The Professional You encompasses your activities that meet the broad definition of the term *work*. They may require travel to an office, store, studio, classroom, or other location to conduct a trade or business. Your work may or may not produce income directly. For example, you could be a stay-at-home parent who does the honorable work of caring for and teaching your children.

   Your Assignment: It's five years from now. You're either still doing work that you love, or you've successfully transitioned from your current work to what you would prefer to do. As you imagine your future, resist placing limitations on how you'll make that transition. Describe your work. Include details about where it's performed and how you feel about it. Why do you enjoy this work? What opportunity does it provide for you? In describing The Professional You, explain how this work answers your need to be productive.

4. **The Financial You.** This part of you keeps track of your money, investments, and financial obligations. It's familiar with savings accounts, payroll taxes, mortgage commitments, income tax returns, and interest rates. The Financial You can read and understand monthly statements from your bank or retirement fund, and interpret that information to decide about future investments. This part requires that you act now to prepare for major financial life events, such as your children attending college or your retirement.

   Your Assignment: Here, you analyze the financial risks in your life and decide the necessary steps to manage those risks so that, in five years, you've put in place the changes you wanted to make. You've completed the prudent financial plan to provide for your future and protect you from unforeseen events. While you'll certainly continue to execute this plan throughout your life, for now, you're justifiably proud that over the last five years you've saved, purchased insurance, and set aside an emergency fund. Write a few paragraphs to a loved one detailing what you've accomplished. Describe The Financial You—the new and improved version.

5. **The Intellectual You.** This part of you constantly seeks fascinating new information. Does The Intellectual You need additional formal education to be satisfied? Or is it content with exploring facts and information from various sources so you don't have to leave your favorite chair? This part of you likes to try new things and seeks new experiences for the knowledge gained. The Intellectual You may want to know how a hybrid vehicle works, how your vote

is counted, or how a jet engine produces enough thrust to keep a heavy airliner aloft for ten hours. It may be curious to learn how foods interact with your bodily systems or what classroom techniques work best for an eight-year-old student. If The Intellectual You isn't fed new information, it becomes bored.

The Intellectual You includes your creative abilities—those parts that want to find expressive outlets, to be free from the bonds of logic and expectations, to just enjoy. The Intellectual You loves to imagine, to solve mysteries and puzzles, to fulfill artistic impulses. Although you might be fortunate to have work that fulfills this need, you may also need a hobby as an outlet. This part of you may like to tinker in the garage repairing broken machinery, combine spices in the kitchen in search of a new and interesting flavor, sing in the church choir, and more.

Your Assignment: It's five years into the future. You're pleased that you've completed the transitions you imagined the first day you started these exercises. You've formed new habits of learning and found fresh ways to express your creativity. Imagine you're sitting with a good friend explaining what you do to satisfy your need for knowledge and creativity. What would you tell this person when describing The Intellectual You? In what ways do you learn something new every day? How do you satisfy your creative impulses?

6. **The Spiritual You.** The Spiritual You—your highest self—includes your core ethical principles. It involves religious beliefs that guide your life as well as your conclusions about existence beyond the physical world. It includes criteria you use in your everyday activities. It also includes rules so fundamental to your life that you don't question them—rules like *help those in need, don't steal, honor your word, and respect others.* The Spiritual You

is that part of you from which inspiration arises—your nonphysical spirit.

Your Assignment: Describe the person you've become five years from now after you've made certain changes to come into alignment with your true spiritual self. How do you think? How do you interact with others? How do you worship? What do you feel? What do you read? How do you spend your time? Describe how your spirit influences your life in the future.

7. **The Psychological You.** Of course, The Psychological You isn't separate from the other six parts. It exists within each of the other parts and is a critical part of you. The Psychological You processes thoughts, makes connections, fills in gaps, creates assumptions, conducts reasoning, and draws conclusions. The Psychological You also includes the emotions you feel, your feelings of happiness, calm, joy, and peace. And it includes how you manage your fears, frustrations, and disappointments. To maintain and exercise this part in a healthy way, uproot and eliminate unhealthy thoughts, flawed reasoning, and hurtful prejudices like you're pulling weeds in a garden.

According to Ralph Waldo Emerson, nineteenth century American essayist, poet, and philosopher, "You become what you think about all day long." I learned this lesson more than twenty years ago and its truth has stayed with me every single day. What I think about, imagine, or believe has an uncanny habit of actually manifesting— maybe not exactly the way I imagined it, but close enough. As a result, I'm meticulous about what I dwell on in my thoughts, and I advise you to be careful, too.

Think intentionally. Think about what you want to experience—and about what you want to become.

Over the next five years, you've identified and dropped any flawed thoughts and beliefs from Step 1 that used to be part of The Psychological You. You've vigilantly built healthy mental habits, cleaned out clutter, and exercised your analytical, logical, and reasoning skills. While you're justifiably proud of the results in your physical, interpersonal, professional, financial, intellectual, and spiritual transformation, you're most pleased about the tremendous progress you've made developing The Psychological You.

Your Assignment: Write down what you've accomplished in the way you think and feel, view the world around you, interpret new information, analyze what you hear, handle challenges, and decide what you say. Include examples of how you've incorporated the choices from Exercise One in this chapter. Fully describe The Psychological You transformed!

WRAPPING IT UP

If you followed the instructions in the seven-part exercise you just completed, you have a written description of the transformed "you" divided into seven short statements. Now put them all together. Take an hour and write down a complete description of who you've become once you've accomplished your goals. If you used a computer, you can cut, paste, and edit. As you do so, notice where the areas overlap.

When you write, continue to resist figuring out how you'll accomplish the changes implicit in your description. Allow yourself to just *be* the person you visualized as you describe yourself to yourself.

Remember, achieving goals starts with having a clear idea of *where you want to go* and *what you want to accomplish.* You just took a major step in that direction. You're well on your way to success.

No doubt you have general thoughts about changes you want to make—be healthier, save more, learn new things, do the work you love, and so on. But if you lack clarity and precision in those goals, they remain fuzzy images off in the distance—wishy-washy wishes rather than solid goals. Being clear and precise is critical to any change and improvement process.

In Step 2 of the *Do What You Can System*, you moved toward clarifying your change goals and closing the gap between what you are and what you *could be*. In completing the two brainstorming and writing exercises in Step 2, you described in far-horizon terms what your life will look like in seven overlapping areas within the next five years. In Step 3 of the *Do What You Can System*, you'll fill in more details for all seven areas.

As you bring clarity and precision to your goals, emphasize the advice given at the close of Chapter One—that is, to suspend ideas, excuses, and other barriers that limit you. As you move from *where you are* and *what you've got* toward *where you want to be* and *who you want to become*, never limit *what you can do*. Give yourself the freedom to dream big and be true to yourself.

Discover, define, and live your purpose.

CHAPTER THREE

FILL IN THE DETAILS

Even on the best day, it takes me a full hour to get from the parking lot to the top of Lovers Leap. Once there, I catch my breath and slow my pulse. After all, the Lovers Leap mountain ridge is more than 10,000 feet above sea level. I lean down to double check that my boots are tightly fastened on the snowboard. Fortunately, I have good equipment—a bright green vintage K-2 Fat Bob snowboard and reliable Flow bindings. (The Fat Bob is a long, wide board made for people like me with big feet and shoes.) Then I stand straight and gauge the constant wind pushing at my back. When it calms down briefly, I shuffle forward in the snow until the toe edge hangs just over the cliff. After a quick glance below, I jump.

I drop only ten feet off the ridge before I make contact with the snow-covered ground, but at age fifty-five, I decide that's a long distance to be unattached to the earth. In what feels like a minute but is likely a fraction of a second, the heel edge of the board catches on the hill behind me. Even though I've made this jump dozens of times, I still feel a flutter of uncertainty and excitement in my chest every time.

After a brief pause to check again that all systems are go, I turn my left shoulder to point straight down the hill and bring my right foot behind me to steer like the rudder on a boat. The physics of gravity and momentum take over. I accelerate quickly, weaving between large boulders through knee-deep powder. The snow explodes around me as I hit that perfect combination of speed, control, and uncertainty. I imagine it's as close to free falling as possible while being in contact with the ground. I hear shouts of pure joy from others flying down the hill a hundred yards to my left.

A minute later, the open terrain changes quickly as I drop into the tree line. The next mile is a constant series of steep drops, sharp turns, and low-hanging branches.

Mistakes are inevitable. Out of numerous attempts over seven winters, I've never completed this run without finding myself upside down in a deep pile of snow because of just one missed turn. Eventually, I come out of the woods and return to the security of a well-groomed, clearly marked ski run. I rendezvous with my wife at the entrance to the next lift, and she helps me remove pine needles and twigs from my goggles and helmet. As she leans close to dig the snow out of the collar of my jacket, she tells me I smell like snow and pine trees. My wide smile says it all. I am indeed a happy man.

Lovers Leap—by far my favorite run at the Vail Ski Resort in Colorado. We're lucky to live only a few miles from the lifts. This proximity gives me endless opportunities to hurl myself into space from the top of that rugged ridge each winter.

But not the winter of 2010. On January 3, at 7 a.m., I had both knees surgically replaced at a hospital in Denver. "Bilateral Knee Arthroplasty," the surgeons called the procedure. I called it "bilateral end of ski season." The replacement operation became necessary due to years of wear and tear from excessive use rather than from any specific incident. I spent most of January on our sofa with ice bags secured by Ace bandages on both elevated knees.

All I could do was jump from Lovers Leap in my mind.

USE VISUALIZATION AS A PLANNING TOOL

Visualization is one of our most powerful life tools. I don't just *believe* this; I *know* it with certainty. As humans, we have the seemingly unbelievable ability to create any image, story, or experience in our minds. I'm talking about conscious visualization—not just the dreams of deep sleep. Wide awake in the middle of the day, we can create in our minds a movie or still picture of anything we choose.

A black-and-white dog. Do you now have an image of a black and white dog in your mind? An orange-and-gold sunset over the ocean. Are you now with me on the beach at dusk? How about a green unicorn?

Anyone can use visualization to recall past experiences. And that's exactly what I did every day as I lay in my living room in the weeks following my knee surgery. I took dozens of runs down Lovers Leap, each time choosing a slightly different course. I even modified my competence level to make it appear as if I were a better snowboarder than I was. What an outstanding athlete I was—at least in *my* mind!

You can just as easily recall past events, modify and edit those experiences, combine multiple related and unrelated events, and play them back in any way you choose. Chances are you do this every day without conscious effort.

Now, pivot that ability 180-degrees—from looking back on your past to looking into your future. Can you use visualization to predict your future? Perhaps not—because planning must take into account a degree of uncertainty. But you *can* use visualization to influence the probability of your results.

I have zero doubt that this works; I've used it successfully for years. I encourage you to suspend any limiting beliefs you may have about the power of visualization to influence what will happen—at least for the time it takes you to complete the exercises in this chapter.

In fact, you've already started using this power. In Step 2, if you completed the assignments to describe yourself five years from now, you used visualization to influence your outcomes. From those exercises in Step 2, if you "see" yourself doing the work you love in the environment you prefer, it's more likely to happen. If you "see" yourself in a loving, secure relationship with your partner, children, parents, or others, this kind of relationship is more likely to manifest. If you "see" your employees working together in a cooperative manner focused on handling customer needs, they're more likely to do just that. With absolute certainty? No. With enhanced probability? Yes—*significantly* enhanced.

A CLEAR AND DETAILED VISION

I've described myself as a fact-based businessperson. An auditor. Analytical and logical. A professional observer of what works and what holds people back. From my years of business experience and many more of life experience, I *know* that having a clear, detailed vision of *what* you want, *where* you want to be, and *who* you want to be dramatically increases the probability these things will manifest.

Remember what Emerson said: "You become what you think about all day long." Implicit in this statement is that the more you think about what you want, the more you bring what you want into reality. The more clarity and feeling you bring to that vision, the better. Here's an example.

One of my favorite vacation activities is sitting on a beach reading a book. Follow me as I build on those experiences and project them into the future with added details.

I see myself sitting in a comfortable cushioned lounge chair on a lava-rock beach on the Big Island of Hawaii. It's midmorning and quiet except for the gentle sound of the warm breeze through the palm trees overhead and the small waves breaking on the black lava rocks. The sun—already high in the cloudless sky—makes the temperature and humidity just right. The air coming off the water brings the slightly salty smell of the ocean wafting toward me. In my left hand, I'm holding a paperback spy mystery so absorbing that I've read at least one hundred pages since I last noticed. In my right hand is a perfect cup of hot Kona coffee. I sip it slowly, savoring its flavor and aroma. Kris sits in the chair next to me, equally absorbed in a crossword puzzle from the morning newspaper. We're completely relaxed, with no plans for the day except to eat lunch and dinner somewhere at some point—when, where, and if we feel like it.

Do you see that by adding details that address all five senses— sight, sound, smell, taste, and touch—the vision comes alive? I now have a clear picture of what I want on a future vacation. As a result, I'll be more open to suggestions that match my vision. When other people talk about their vacations, I'll be especially attentive if the discussion includes a beach area. Down the road when it comes time to make travel decisions, the image I created will have an effect on where I go. No doubt I'll notice the specials on Hawaii offered in the paper. When Kris asks me for my vacation ideas, you can probably guess what I'll suggest.

Detailed visualization works with all seven life areas from the Step 2 exercise. In your work environment, when you describe your perfect day using as many senses as possible, the image of your ideal work situation comes alive. For example, you may see yourself working in an office just ten minutes from your home, or you may be doing creative community service work each day. Perhaps you visualize yourself surrounded by coworkers and supervisors who enjoy their work and each other's company. The more detail you add to your vision—the benefits from your work, where your office is located, how your coworkers interact, exactly what you're doing, and more—the clearer the vision becomes and the more likely it will actually occur. It will certainly move you in that direction.

Do you have teenage children? If so, imagine the details of your perfect relationship with them. See yourselves talking freely and honestly with one another, sitting down to share meals of high-quality food—without the TV distracting you. Imagine a relationship in which teens and adults willingly share the chores around the house. Visualize a positive attitude based on love, trust, accountability, mutual understanding, and clear expectations. Also see yourself modeling appropriate parental behavior, which gets rewarded with appropriate teen behavior.

Again, the more detail you add to your vision, the clearer it becomes and the more likely it will happen. Isn't it logical? Compare that to having no detailed vision or—worse still—a negative one. To quote Dr. Wayne Dyer, "What you think about expands."

In my seminars, I talk about the power of visualization to increase the likelihood of desired outcomes. About 70 percent of the attendees nod in agreement; 20 percent cock their heads slightly with questions in their eyes; the remaining 10 percent look at me as if I'm trying to sell them poison.

Please know I'm not trying to sell anything except *action ideas* derived from observing others—ideas I've implemented in my life and my work. For me, they work exceedingly well. And they'll likely work for you, too. Don't discount or dismiss that possibility without attempting them!

As with all new ideas, try them first in a limited, safe manner. If they feel right and give you the results you want, expand how you use them. If, after a trial period, they don't feel right, you have a legitimate reason to drop them from your toolbox.

Right now, pick a person who's important to you but your relationship is unsatisfactory to you. Take five minutes and write down how that relationship would look if it were perfect. List details like these: the tone of the words when speaking with this person; how and where you spend time together; what you'd like him or her to say to you. Also write down *why* this relationship is important to you. Then "see" it in a new way, feel it differently, hear new interactions in your mind. As you describe it, be clear and specific.

The next time you speak to this person, remember what you wrote. Better still, while this exercise is fresh in your thoughts, visit or call the person. Be proactive. Do this consistently and regularly over several weeks. Observe if the concerns you harbored begin to disappear or at least improve. In fact, make it a *priority* to find out.

Gaining a quick win with visualization can ease your concerns and encourage you to use it again in other areas of your life.

STEP 3: ADD DETAILS TO EACH VISION

In Step 2, you created a written statement of what you would look like in five years when you've completed all of the changes you want. Your written results covered seven areas of your life—the physical, interpersonal, professional, financial, intellectual, spiritual, and psychological parts of you. With the notes from that exercise, go back and add details to each vision, just as I did with my day at the beach. Use as many senses as possible.

For example, in the section on The Physical You, I stated my intention to be in "excellent health" in five years. Next, I would add details to create a vision of what excellent health means for a sixty-year-old me. I would color in that vision with data that can be measured, including weight, body mass index, blood pressure, heart rate, and cholesterol readings.

I also stated my intention to "eat in a healthy manner, focusing on the quality and source of what I consume." It's time to color in the details of that simple statement. For example, my resolve is to take the following actions:

- *Seek out and eat food certified as organic.*
- *Eat several servings of fresh fruits and vegetables every day.*
- *Know the source of any animal products I consume.*
- *Avoid any food containing unhealthy chemicals or other additives.*
- *Read food package labels in stores and research the implications of each ingredient included in the product.*

(This can be frustrating at first, but stay with it. A little research on the purpose of each added ingredient will improve your buying decisions significantly.)

- *Ask restaurant staff about the source of my food, how it's prepared, and what's been added during preparation.*

Details like these add color, clarity, and substance to your vision. Taking time to think them through and write them down reinforces your vision while increasing the likelihood that you'll act in support of these goals.

Reward yourself with quiet time and do nothing except fill in the details of your vision of your fully transformed self. Use strong positive terms. Address all seven areas from the exercises you did in Chapter Two.

Also, carry a notebook for one full week. Each day, pick one of the seven life areas and, throughout the day, keep that area in your thoughts. Write down details as they occur to you. At the end of the week, you'll have a comprehensive description of all seven areas.

SHARING YOUR INTENTIONS

So far, you've been instructed to create a compelling, detailed vision for yourself. However, keeping your plans to yourself saves you from hearing any criticism or doubt from others. And by keeping them private, you can easily change the details of your vision to reflect changing circumstances, new information, or any other factors. You just act on them without fanfare or the need for approval.

However, it may be advantageous to share your vision with the right people for the following reasons:

- *Explaining your vision and goals aloud helps you clarify your thoughts. When you share what you intend to accomplish, you're forced to be clear in the words you use*

> *and therefore more careful and specific in describing your desired results.*
>
> - *When others you trust hear your plans, their questions and comments can uncover any fuzzy or incomplete details in your vision, thus helping you to be thorough.*
>
> - *People who hear your plans may have just the right thought or suggestion to help you with the how part. You may hear comments such as, "I know someone who might be a big help," or "I'll tell you where I went for that kind of result."*
>
> - *Telling others about your plans reinforces your intentions and builds your level of commitment.*

If you're stuck in your visualization, need a little push, or just want to practice saying your goals out loud, explain them to someone you trust. Be sure to pick a confidant who will be supportive. In addition, choose the timing of those discussions wisely.

Word of caution: Take your visualization as far as you can on your own to avoid being prematurely influenced by others.

A SUGGESTION ON VISUALIZATION FOR BUSINESS LEADERS

Throughout my career, I've observed situations in which supervisors and employees were ready, willing, and able to perform whatever was asked of them. Unfortunately, senior managers failed to be specific about what they wanted. They didn't help their employees "see" and "feel" what was needed. Issuing guidelines and setting performance targets from above, they failed to fill in the vivid details of the exact desired results. They also failed to define what excellent customer service looks like, nor were they specific about how to treat coworkers and subordinates. They threw around the term *teamwork* without describing what a smoothly working team looks like. In short, they didn't use the power of visual examples to create a compelling picture of what they wanted.

When this happens (and it continues to do so), leaders seem surprised when their team members—specifically their staff and supervisors—don't deliver on expectations that were never adequately explained in the first place. In organizations, both large and small, this vicious circle can become the norm, with leaders issuing broad statements of goals and expectations without clear details, and supervisors and staff incorrectly interpreting what's wanted.

In their book *Switch*, Chip and Dan Heath stress the importance of "scripting the critical moves." They write: ". . . the hardest part of change—the paralyzing part—is precisely in the details."[1] They also note: "To spark movement in a new direction, you need to provide crystal-clear direction. That's why scripting [details] is so important—you've got to think about the specific behavior that you'd want to see. . . ."[2]

Here's an example from one of my favorite clients. The vice president of sales called an all-hands meeting to discuss the five key components of the company's customer service program. With every sales representative present in the room, she worked through the five main points of the program. When addressing each one, she used the power of real-life examples indicating both good service and poor service. She explained exactly how she wanted each sales representative to act when in contact with customers. She described probable interactions in detail, suggesting scripted responses to customer questions. Then she conducted a ten-minute role-play exercise to show and reinforce the behavior she expected from everyone present. Following that, every sales representative in the room did a similar role-play. Working in small teams, each person received input on their performance during the exercise and suggestions reinforcing their positive results. The vice president then took questions from the reps for more than an hour, investing this time to answer every question with an example that illustrated the desired customer service behavior.

The vice president's words and detailed examples created a vision of good service in everyone's mind. She did a beautiful job! Yes, it took time to prepare and deliver this program, but the result was incredible. The sales staff knew not only what the boss wanted but *exactly how to do* what she wanted.

The message? If you're in a leadership position at any level in your organization, provide clear, detailed examples of what you want from your team. Demonstrate exactly what you want done. Use succinct, specific language. Be visual in your instructions. Remember, the human mind works in pictures.

Whenever possible, do it in person so people can ask questions and get clarifications. Emails and PowerPoint slides can be efficient, but generally these communication methods don't encourage the use of vivid visual examples and they don't provide an effective forum for clarifying questions and dialogue.

Test it and see how it works for you.

In *The 7 Habits of Highly Effective People*, author Stephen R. Covey encourages readers to fully engage in the power of visualization. On Covey's website, habit number two, *Begin with the End in Mind*, is based on imagination—the ability to envision in your mind what you cannot see. Also stated on the website:

> . . . *all things are created twice. There is a mental (first) creation, and a physical (second) creation. The physical creation follows the mental, just as a building follows a blueprint. If you don't make a conscious effort to visualize who you are and what you want in life, then you empower other people and circumstances to shape you and your life by default.*[3]

By following the *Do What You Can System*, you claim the power to define your own goals. In Steps 2 and 3, you follow the advice of Covey and others by defining them with the end in mind—the next horizon of your life.

As stated earlier, having a clear, consistent vision of your desired result increases the likelihood of achieving that result. Does my writing about it make it true for you? No. So is it real? Yes. I've used this process so often, I *know* it works. As a result, I'm now extremely careful what I wish for and think about.

"I'll believe it when I see it" is a cliché, but it's true and it works. Oddly enough, the opposite is also true as witnessed by Dr. Wayne Dyer, who wrote *You'll See It When You Believe It*. Here's how it works: *Seeing* (visualizing) something ahead of time and *believing* (knowing) it will happen makes *doing* much more likely, which increases the probability.

To recap: See your results in your mind, state them in positive visual terms, be specific, and keep reinforcing the image mentally. Move from stating general targets (e.g., be a better spouse, get thin, quit smoking) to visualizing specific details. For example, visualize yourself buying your wife flowers, washing her car, cleaning the house. Picture yourself buying clothes a size smaller and feel the joy of seeing a slimmer you in the mirror. Feel the satisfaction of observing that your breath, clothing, house, and car no longer smell of cigarette smoke. For a stronger effect, engage all of your senses in your visualizations.

At the same time, avoid negative thoughts, limiting beliefs, and incomplete images. Remember, *you* are responsible for your thoughts and thus "response-able" for your results.

Give yourself plenty of time to write out a clear, detailed vision of your changed self. Resist the urge to move on to Step 4 until you've completed the visualization and writing exercises in Steps 2 and 3. They form your foundation.

CHAPTER FOUR

CREATE YOUR ACTION PLAN

In September 2010, I took an action that changed everything in my business. Until that time, I was consistently busy consulting and giving presentations seventy-five to one hundred times each year. Some were a few hours; most were all-day seminars. The presentations delivered valuable content in my areas of technical skill—business effectiveness, process improvement, internal controls, and fraud prevention. But doing them meant taking about one hundred flights and staying about two hundred nights in hotel rooms every year. For business people other than dedicated road warriors, this routine is unusual, but it's normal for full-time speakers and consultants like myself.

However, for as long as I can remember, I have always wanted to write and speak on personal and business *transformation*. In my travels, I observed organizations doing important work and operating at peak levels. I saw people who loved their careers and pursued them with passion and energy. I read countless articles and books about peak performance. From each experience, I sought to understand *how* people obtained outstanding results and *why* they loved what they did.

For ten years, I kept a folder of ideas that grew into a two-inch-thick mess of unorganized Post-it notes, torn-out articles, and barely readable scribbled messages. The business and self-help books I accumulated occupied four full shelves in my office. But that's as far as I got.

The fall of 2010 marked the official twentieth anniversary of my speaking and consulting career—a long commitment and important intersection like the type discussed in Chapter One. At fifty-five years old and facing at least another ten years of hard work before retirement, I took my own advice from Step 1.

When I stopped, looked, and listened, I arrived at these important conclusions:

- *I enjoy my core work of speaking and consulting.*
- *I have above-average speaking skills from giving nearly 2,000 presentations.*
- *I spend too many nights away from home in hotels.*
- *I'm not taking full advantage of technology as I do my work.*
- *I want to shift my core presentation and consulting work to my Do What You Can System.*

That was the genesis of this book.

A STEP TOWARD THE FUTURE

To move toward what I wanted, I took this crucial step in September 2010: I attended a monthly meeting of the local chapter of the National Speakers Association (NSA). I'd been a member of NSA ten years before but had drifted away as my career changed. I'd forgotten how valuable a resource membership and active participation had been at that time. Attending that September 2010 meeting and rejoining this association may have been the most critical event of my entire speaking career. Let me explain why.

At the Saturday morning gathering held at a hotel in the Denver area, round tables filled the ballroom, with six chairs to a table. Coffee and other refreshments lined tables in the back of the room; a raised temporary stage, projector, and screen were up front. Busy setting up the sound system, Internet connections, and cameras was just one man. As he moved quickly, it looked like he needed to focus on what he was doing, so I stayed out of the way and networked with others coming in the door. At the designated start time, I did what many people do at my own seminars—I chose a table off to the side.

The meeting began with a welcome from our master of ceremonies—the same man who had set up the staging—Orvel Ray Wilson. Orvel Ray isn't a name one forgets. And I was certain I had heard it before. In his comments, he mentioned that several chapter members he coached were at the meeting. As we clapped to welcome the first speaker, I reviewed what I'd quickly learned about him. In charge of meeting room set up, master of ceremonies, and professional speaker coach. Interesting. Then, to my surprise, he sat down right next to me!

We introduced ourselves and I wondered aloud why his name was so familiar. He asked if I knew his book *Guerrilla Selling*. In a flash of recognition, I thought, "Yes. He's the author of an outstanding book on using 'unconventional weapons and tactics for increasing your sales.'" He's also well known as a world-class speaker and sales trainer. Besides that, I remembered his book had a place on a shelf in my office.

Over the next nine months, what began as a serendipitous sharing at a meeting blossomed into a full-scope mentoring relationship. During this time, I moved ten years of stalled intentions into full action. In our twice-monthly meetings, we covered these items:

- *Understanding the business of speaking*
- *Finding new clients*

- *Providing better service to existing clients*
- *Using the power of technology and the Internet to advance my speaking career*
- *Delivering more effective live presentations*
- *Using video and audio recordings to reach a wider audience*

In our meetings that continue to this day, Orvel Ray pushes and challenges, instructs and critiques. He helps eliminate blocks on the way to fulfilling dreams. Without his support, the book you're reading would still be a two-inch folder of scraps and Post-it notes. Thanks to my work with him, I pulled ten-plus years of good intentions into a comprehensive plan of action—one that I call the *Do What You Can System.*

YOUR PROGRESS SO FAR

Using *The System* as your guide, you too can move yourself to action with what *you* have. At this point in *The System*, you have already looked hard at where you are and where you want to go. In Step 1, you listed the skills you've developed and will build on as you move confidently toward your goals. You also looked at the heavy anchors and excuses from your past—the ones you're still dragging around that do nothing but slow you down, destroy your momentum, and burn up your precious energy.

In Step 2, you created a far-horizon vision of where you want to be in five years. You wrote a description of your desired end state, covering seven key areas of your life.

In Step 3, you used visualization to add details to those descriptions.

At this point, you should also have a detailed written description of what you want to accomplish plus a list of skills from your past. If you've given your attention to these first three steps, you've already invested several hours, even several days, in *The System*. You've accomplished much and are well on your way to achieving your goals.

Now, you're probably eager to stop planning and start taking action. But you'll need to take one more critical step first—Step 4. In this step, you convert your thoughts, ideas, and vision into an achievable plan of action. Then in Step 5, you'll execute that plan.

Before you work on your action plan, a reminder: The seven life areas from Step 2 don't stand alone; they overlap substantially. So any action plan for growth must address them both individually and as a whole.

In Step 4, you'll take another look at the seven areas individually, but when they are combined, they must work as an integrated whole rather than separate strategies. The concept echoes a business marketing campaign that includes television advertising, print ads, in-person contact by sales reps, and Internet presence. Each component operates separately and simultaneously yet is directed to one common goal. You'll take action on each of the seven areas every day. That way, you'll progress on all seven fronts at the same time to accomplish your full objective.

MAKE A PLAN TO MEET YOUR PURPOSE

Step 4 requires you to build on Steps 2 and 3 and write your plan of action, incorporating the skills and abilities you identified in Step 1. You define your sources of assistance (which may include your own mentor or coach) to close the gaps between what you *have been doing* and what you *can* do.

A CONCEPTUAL FOUNDATION

Before you dig into the details of creating your plan, let's address these three interrelated concepts: leverage, mentors, and the multiplier effect. You'll increase the speed and quality of your change efforts when you use these concepts:

1. Take full advantage of the leverage available from *all* information (experience, experts, books, the Internet, and other sources) and *all* forces (energy, flow, and momentum). By definition, leverage increases output for each unit of input. That means it multiplies your own abilities through additional resources.

2. Build formal relationships with mentors, coaches, and others who already know how to do what you want to do.

3. Multiply what you can accomplish alone by combining leverage (resources) with a coach/mentor relationship (the multiplier effect).

Let's look at an example of each.

Using leverage in your life works like the natural energy of falling water pushing a large wheel in an old mill. This motion turns a shaft that operates a grindstone or machine. Likewise, through the leverage effect of hydraulics, you can safely stop a vehicle weighing several tons by depressing the brake pedal with one foot. The multiplying energy of seemingly small technological additions to a task can exponentially add effectiveness. That's the power of leverage.

In my career, I leveraged the information I gleaned from NSA, books, webinars, speakers, and other sources to increase the effectiveness of my own skills and knowledge. As you consider how to implement your changes, don't start from scratch. It's wise to leverage *existing information* and *proven processes* to accelerate your results.

Regarding the power of mentoring and coaching, I've described the tremendous boost I received from my relationship with Orvel Ray Wilson. With the benefit of his experience-based knowledge and proven techniques, I've achieved in nine months what would have taken me several years on my own. I'm competent, but he's an expert. Together, we're building the specific structure I needed in my business around information I'd obtained from other sources. Combining the leveraging effect of information with the focusing effect of working with a qualified coach, I've multiplied my results several times over. And so can you. After several months of working with Orvel Ray, my expanded speaking calendar covers new and exciting topics (including the material in this book), my revenue has increased significantly, and most important of all, my speaking skills have moved to a higher level.

These concepts—leverage, mentors, and the multiplier effect—are the foundation on which you'll build a detailed plan of action.

CREATING ACTION PLANS THAT WORK

Most people want to improve their lives—lose weight, get in better physical shape, move their careers to the next level, secure their financial position, or improve their relationships. Many want to adjust many areas at once, even go for a complete overhaul.

I applaud all efforts to improve. Yet I see repeatedly how well-intentioned people fail to achieve their goals because of breakdowns in how they implement their plans. They lack a *system* that keeps their activities on track. Consequently, they

- *exercise for a week or two, and then stop;*
- *make an effort to be more attentive to family members but get busy with other priorities and let this one drop off; and*
- *save a small amount of money from a few paychecks but fail to cut back on discretionary credit card spending.*

Many people—myself included—fall victim to the "shiny red ball syndrome." We're easily distracted from our goals by something "shiny" that catches our attention. For example, we intend to go for a long walk but turn on the television first and get caught up in a movie or sports program. That walk never happens. We intend to make plans for Saturday night to dine out with our partner but get busy with a work project and fail to reserve a table or find someone to watch the children. We plan to attend religious services on the weekend, but the cozy bed wins; when the alarm sounds, we roll over and go back to sleep.

Yes, we have great intentions but fail to implement because we become distracted. For many, distraction is a deeply ingrained habit. Breaking that habit can be like trying to chop down hardwood trees.

How do successful people handle this human tendency? *They create a tightly closed system of specific actions that increase the probability of success.* Then they execute this system every day until they've replaced old habits with new, more effective actions. Consciously and with precision, they define *what* they will do, *why* they will do it, *how* they will do it, and *when* they will do it.

Let's consider in detail five things successful people do that will assist you in your own endeavors. They are integral to the *Do What You Can System*.

1. **Successful people match their existing skills (Step 1) with a detailed visualization of their desired end state (Steps 2 and 3).** They analyze the skills, tools, and resources they need to accomplish their goals and then act to close the gaps between what they *have* and what they *need*. They fully consider the what, when, and how of their plans, recognizing that the skills and resources they need in one area of growth (financial) may be different from what they need in another area (spiritual). They constantly ask, "How can I make this possible?" and then find or develop the resources they need to accomplish their goals. They also ask, "Does this make sense?" They're not afraid to revise their goals as needed.

   Although successful people believe in research, research, and more research, they don't let analysis be an excuse for failure to act. Nor do they allow themselves to get analysis paralysis; rather, they act as soon as possible on what they learn. They realize the importance of relevant information. They ask qualified people what they think and know without making assumptions. Open-minded and flexible, they're not afraid to revise their assessment of their existing skills, their vision of the desired results, and the resources needed.

Practical and methodical in their approach, successful people align their goals, methods, and environment as well as the actions of people whose help they need. In support of this alignment, they're careful to build a clear and consistent description of their intentions, both for themselves and for communicating their needs to others (Step 3). What's more, they understand that their main resource consists of their own efforts. Therefore, they consciously improve their skills, tend to their own needs, and maintain their bodies and minds. At the same time, they willingly leave behind any habits that impede their progress.

Here's an example from a recent experience. When we began working together, my coach and I started by defining specific goals for my business and a general time line for action. From that, we defined the specific actions to be taken and the measures we would use to gauge results. We included details about other experts who might help and a plan on how to solicit that help. We discussed the "environmental" factors that either assist or get in the way, including organization of my workspace, computer, audio and video equipment needs, and books on writing and speaking skills to fill in the gaps in my knowledge. Last, we determined how to allocate time in my day to allow an uninterrupted two hours early each morning—before handling or even touching anything else—dedicated to the tasks that *needed* to be done that day to keep the plan on track. Our overall goals? Define the desired results in my skill building and business building, identify the gaps between the starting and end points, and spell out a specific plan to move me in the right direction.

2. **Successful people identify and assemble a support team.** Knowing that someone has already done what they intended to do—and done it well—they set out to find those people and ask for help. They understand that it's easier and more efficient than doing it alone. They remember the core ideas—leverage, mentors, and the multiplier effect— proving that having a network saves legwork.

   Following their lead, where do you find the skilled people you need? First, ask, "Do I already know someone who could help me with this?" Then ask others for ideas and referrals. You might join a club or association to network with experts and others who are on the same path.

   Seek different advisors for each area of your goals. For example, to improve your physical condition, you require an expert in exercise and conditioning who's knowledgeable in diet and nutrition. Or you may need to find two or more experts. Think in terms of your support *team;* different growth areas require different skills and therefore different team members.

   For your career growth, pay attention at work. Who has the legitimate respect of senior management? What do they do to earn that respect? Approach these people and ask for suggestions.

   For your psychological growth, pay attention each day to those around you who seem happy and healthy in their thoughts. Spend time with them to find out how they maintain their inner peace in this crazy world. Ask them what they read, how they spend their free time, how they address stressful situations, and how they bring their positive approach to life's challenges.

For your spiritual growth, ask those you perceive to be more adept at spiritual matters than you are at present. Seek out mentors at your place of worship.

For your financial growth, recruit a qualified financial advisor—one who's willing to take the time to understand your goals and will help you build a plan to accomplish those goals.

Ideally, everyone on your support team has the following attributes:

- *Subject matter expertise*
- *Availability when needed (within reason, of course)*
- *Willingness to provide honest, objective input and feedback*
- *Ability to challenge your assumptions, actions, and progress*
- *Empathetic encouragement*
- *Full belief in you and your goals*

After identifying your resource team members, be ready to state your goals in clear, specific, visual terms. Address the what, why, how, and when details of your intentions. Write down these details, one page for each area, and share the relevant page with each team member. Frame their thinking by telling them exactly what you intend to accomplish. Help them see themselves in your situation so they can assist in creating the *how* of your approach.

Be sure to offer something of value to them. This could be your availability to counsel, analyze, and encourage them in their own endeavors. Or it could be a financial incentive (for your financial advisors, physical conditioning coaches, and educational specialists, for example). In short, understand your desired results and then ask for the specific help you need.

By building a support team, you're not creating from scratch. Rather, you're assembling experts who already exist. Be like successful people who find the experts they need to achieve their goals and then pull them into the process. Doing so maximizes the big three: leverage, mentors, and the multiplier effect.

Review your Step 3 descriptions of the changes you intend to make. In each area of growth, identify where you need expert help. What subject matter experts would accelerate your progress if they were a part of your support team? Find them, ask for their help as described here, and offer something they value in return.

3. **In determining *how* they will accomplish their goals, successful people are aggressively attentive to deliverables, deadlines, and measures.** They define what they want to accomplish and how they will measure their results. Then they set tough deadlines. However, they also build in flexibility to accommodate new information and changing circumstances. They revise their deadlines rather than drop them to keep their plan on track. While flexible in their approach, they don't waver from pursuing what they want.

The core concepts of deliverables, deadlines, and measures are largely self-evident. For each area of personal improvement, you identify specific deliverables or targets based on your desired end goal, with interim subgoals along the way. For example, if your goal is to lose twenty-five pounds in six months, that deliverable (weight loss) has a stated deadline (six months) and is measurable (twenty-five pounds). You can set up interim deliverables, deadlines, and measures over those six months.

At the end of the first month and for the end of each successive month, you set a sub-goal of losing four pounds (one pound a week). This goal easily lends itself to measures of progress (or shortfalls) at interim dates during the six-month period. A goal of walking a mile each day can also be easily measured as well as intentions of eating a set number of servings of vegetables or fruit each day.

Granted, some areas of transformation don't lend themselves to easy measurement. In the areas of interpersonal and psychological growth, for example, setting deadlines and then accurately measuring progress toward your goals can be challenging. Yet successful people find a way to do it. They set up deliverables, deadlines, and measures for all their important goals—physical, interpersonal, professional, financial, intellectual, spiritual, and psychological. Being creative in how they measure their spiritual, interpersonal, and psychological growth, they rely on questions such as, "What have I done today to become more aligned with my spiritual self?" Then they reflect on their day, looking for examples of progress or setbacks.

More important, successful people continually look for ways to set and balance the deadlines in all of their growth areas. Although they're not slaves to a rigid plan, they're attentive to daily movement forward on all of their growth goals.

Look again at the descriptions you prepared in Step 3. Take time *right now* to determine specific targets for each area. Then establish immediate (this week), short-term (six months), and long-term (five years) deliverables, deadlines, and measures. The results become a critical part of your written growth plan.

4. **Successful people commit their plans to writing.** I learned this lesson on my first day with a company twenty-five years ago when my supervisor asked, "John, do you

have a career plan? Show it to me!" Of course, I had no written career plan. Or financial plan. Or spiritual plan. Or any other plan that looked beyond the upcoming weekend or summer vacation.

In my work with companies today, I see that most of the business units I've reviewed had no credible plan for growth, action, or contingencies. At a higher organizational level, a strategic plan covering three to five years of intended actions and results may have existed. But at the operating unit level, detailed written plans to guide execution were a rare exception.

This goes for individuals, too. Few people have a detailed idea of their short- and long-term plans for career, finances, psychological and creative growth, or any of the seven life areas emphasized in this book. In hindsight, I've learned that failing to set career plans or track progress decreases the probability of success.

In contrast, written plans can

- *remind you of the actions needed to move forward in a logical manner,*

- *help you avoid beliefs and behaviors that can hold you back,*

- *focus your attention and actions,*

- *direct how you invest your time,*

- *guide you in moments of decision, and*

- *remind you what's important when you might otherwise be distracted.*

When urgent matters push aside the important issues documented in your plan, your written plan can put you back on track quickly once the urgent matter gets handled.

5. **Successful people build in flexibility, fun, and balance.**
    Isn't growing and pursuing your goals supposed to be enjoyable? Are you to follow your written plans, deadlines, deliverables, and measures so rigidly, they become another burden in your already hectic life? I believe it should indeed feel pleasurable to advance in the direction of your dreams. Otherwise why do it? Make it fun!

    Your written plans aren't meant to rule your life. Instead, they provide a guide and an incentive to keep moving toward that dream you see so vividly and want so much.

    You set the goals and the methods to accomplish them; no one else does it for you. Any pressure you feel, you're putting on yourself. Remember what was said in the Introduction? *For this process to work, you need to acknowledge that you and you alone are responsible for your results.*

    Fortunately, many of the changes you plan to make can be woven into other activities through the day. For example, you can improve your interpersonal skills during meetings you'll attend anyway. You needn't extend the meeting to practice your skills; just be more attentive to how you listen and communicate while you're in the meeting. In fact, you are wise to work at being more clear and concise in your statements throughout the day. Make it an interesting challenge to do so.

    As you complete your work of drafting emails and other documents, be sure to focus on improving your writing. For spiritual and psychological growth, take a few minutes between tasks and clear your thoughts of clutter. Be aware of how a short period of calm in the middle of a busy day not only helps you become more aligned with your spiritual self, but it enables you to focus on your next task.

Build balance into your plans. Blend the action steps of your *Do What You Can System* into your normal routine. Take small but noticeable steps toward *all* of your identified goals. You'll find having a written plan of deliverables, deadlines, and measures that balances existing realities and responsibilities makes the changes easier to assimilate into your daily behavior.

STEP 4: WRITE YOUR PLAN

Now it's time to dig in and write! Here are ten ideas to get you started and more suggestions to keep you going.

1. Yes, your plan must be in writing. If it's not written, it's not a plan.

2. Address each intended area of life change, growth, or transformation separately (the seven areas covered in this book plus any others you'd like to add). Design a plan for each goal so it stands on its own but aligns in format with your plans in every other goal area. The combined plan should be read as one clear, thorough, and consistent plan of action. In your plan for growth, include details about

   - *what the results of your intended changes or transformation will be,*

   - *how you will accomplish those changes,*

   - *the skills you bring to the effort,*

   - *mentors and coaches who will help,*

   - *interim and ultimate deadlines for the completion of your plan, and*

   - *how you will measure progress along the way and determine successful completion of each goal.*

3. Let your plan document for each area run several pages covering all suggested points. For example, if you devote four pages to each of the seven life change areas suggested, you'll write close to thirty pages. Stay with it until it feels complete. After all, you're designing your life!

4. Include specific measurable goals for five years, one year (updated annually), one month (updated monthly), and one week (updated—you get it—weekly).

5. Use bullet points and lists because they're generally easier to skim and review than long paragraphs.

6. Start at the end with the visualized image of your desired change from Step 3. Work back to the present, identifying the needed steps along the way.

7. Be realistic. Set targets that can be accomplished without ignoring your existing commitments and other realities in your life.

8. Every day, create checklists to keep you on track. Include at least one specific action for each area of targeted growth. At the end of each day, review your progress on that day's list of actions and update your to-do list for the following day. Enjoy the feeling of accomplishment when you cross off completed items. Treat these checklists as scorecards of morning intentions and evening results.

9. If possible, use a computer and word processing software to document your plan. It's easy to do revisions and week-ly, monthly, and annual updates using these tools.

10. Take your time in writing the initial plan. It will cover a lot of detail, so break the task down into manageable chunks. Devote forty-five minutes to an hour at a time for brainstorming and writing. If you hit a mental block, walk away and try again later. Maintaining a clear mind and re-freshed body is especially helpful while brainstorming. Be

open to investing a week or more in the process of drafting your original plan that covers five years into the future. Think intentionally as you write and don't rush.

Review or skim through your entire plan every few days. This will remind you about your long-term targets and clarify how your actions that day (and every day) will take you in that direction.

Why so much attention to creating and document-ing a detailed plan? Easy answer. People acting with or-ganized, well-planned systems are efficient, while people acting without a coordinated plan are not. A daily struc-tured routine is surprisingly effective in helping you reach your targeted results. And of course set your targets in the first place—or you won't know where to aim.

KEEP A POSITIVE PERSPECTIVE

Yes, counterproductive habits will get in the way at first. No need to interrupt them all at the same time. Instead, break them gradu-ally but consistently as you proceed. Forming new ones can be sat-isfying if you can stay positive—even if it doesn't go well at first.

Indeed, keep a positive perspective about all your failures, no matter what they are. Many writers, speakers, and philosophers are on record as saying there's no such thing as failure—only op-portunities to improve. Many statements about failure are attributed to nineteenth-century American inventor Thomas Edison with a theme that each failed experiment brought him closer to success. While I agree with these statements in general, I fear they downplay the toll of trying hard but coming up short. When I experienced failures in my life, few could be called fun (even though I learned from them).

What's my "favorite" failure? In the winter of 1973, my high school English teacher volunteered me for the minor role of Dr.

Maguire in our school's stage production of *Look Homeward Angel*. My teacher thought it would be a great stretch goal for me. Stretch indeed. I had never done anything like that before.

This Pulitzer Prize winning play is a comedy-drama in three acts based on the novel by Thomas Wolfe. It's set in 1916 in a Dixieland Boarding House, a flimsy frame house of fifteen draughty rooms in Altamont, North Carolina. The house "has a rambling, unplanned appearance, and is painted a dirty yellow."[1] How's that for a motivating visual image?

In the play, the thirty-year-old hero, Ben, has tuberculosis, (known at the time as "consumption"), and just before the curtain falls on the second act, Ben experiences a series of spasms and deep coughs and then dies. Dr. Maguire—yours truly—oversees this critical moment as Ben—played by my friend Bob—passes from this world to the next. It's a solemn moment intended to focus on the pain experienced by family members when they lose their beloved son. As Ben draws his last raspy breath, coughs twice, and becomes still, I say this one line confirming that Ben has passed: "It's over. It's all over." Solemnly delivered, followed by silence.

The audience burst into laughter. Here I am, seventeen years old, on the brightly lit center stage in our school's large auditorium. It's the critical transition moment in a dramatic production, I've just pronounced the death of the star, and the audience is *laughing*. Forty years later, I still have no idea why. My mother, who was in the audience, could only tell me, "John, when you said that line—it was just funny."

The curtain fell and the stage went dark. I stood up and walked quickly into the shadows. As I passed the director—another teacher at the school—he shot me a look of absolute rage. On the spot, I made a promise to myself. *I will never speak in public again.* Four decades later, I'm a professional.

Was it fun to fail miserably on the well-lit stage in front of hundreds of people? No, absolutely not. Later, when I could finally look back with a positive perspective, here's what I concluded. As a speaker, I could *never* fail that miserably again. I'm just glad I got it out of my system early in my career!

Some say the deepest learning comes from doing it wrong, which is true but only if you get up, dust yourself off, and try again until you get it right.

Bottom line for you? Build flexibility and balance into your plans and *expect* failure. Plan to both avoid and quickly recover from mistakes and missteps. Build in fun, even when things don't go according to plan. Just say, "Well, I'm glad I got *that* out of my system!" Recalibrate your intentions as you progress, moving forward each day and enjoying the journey.

No need to sprint and burn out. For example, don't shortchange the restorative effect of sleep by forcing yourself to read spiritual texts at night when you're exhausted. Don't run a mile when you're only physically capable of walking. Just walk that mile and smile as you do. Be flexible but persistent.

In one of my early mentoring sessions with Orvel Ray, he asked me why I hadn't written this book after ten years of collecting ideas and putting them in a folder. I offered these lame excuses: "I'm still thinking about it. Not enough time in the day. Not sure if there's an audience. It's all been said before. . . ." He challenged me, saying these were all excuses to avoid doing the writing work. Then he issued this simple instruction: "Send me one line every day. Even just one word. But do it every day."

He kept nudging me about this commitment. He'd send emails reminding me he hadn't received anything in a few days. So finally I sat down with my laptop computer and started to write—about anything at first. Within a week or two, I had roughly outlined this book on three sheets of paper. I set aside a full day one cold January weekend and organized the notes in my thick folder. I pledged to start each morning at my desk or in a hotel room with a cup of coffee and at least fifteen minutes of writing. Most days, those fifteen minutes grew into a full hour before I realized it. Three months later, I had finished the first draft of Chapters One through Four. It happened one line at a time.

My advice? Get started. Pledge the equivalent of at least one simple action daily toward each of your stated goals. Find your own accountability coach—someone who will nudge you gently but consistently and say, "Did you take that one step today?"

You started Chapter Four with a clear, detailed vision of what you want to accomplish and ended with a comprehensive written plan of action to bring about the life changes you desire.

Your plan includes the leveraging resources you'll need (including mentors and coaches), how you will accomplish your goals, when you intend to achieve them, and how you will measure your progress and determine your success. Congratulations!

Now get ready for action, action, and more action. Catch your breath and review your plan to date. Then write out tomorrow's to-do list and get a good night's sleep.

Tomorrow is Day One of your transformation—a very big day.

TIME TO ACT!

Pencils down! Computer off! Step 5 is about action.

Finally, after all the deep thinking and writing you've done, it's time to make your plan come to life. By completing the first four steps of the *Do What You Can System,* you've shown you have a strong desire to change your life and pursue your goals. Important change requires that you reprogram your thinking, revise your habits, and consciously adjust many of your daily actions.

Unfortunately, some people don't want to change. Not even a little. They think about it, and they may even talk about the changes they intend to make. But they don't act.

ARE YOU LIKE THESE PEOPLE?

As you read about Tony and Frank, are you seeing aspects of yourself in the mirror?

TONY

Tony, a fellow passenger on a recent flight, is one resistant guy. I learn that he's a businessman on his way home from a busy week of work-related travel. A large man by his own admission, he mentions how he struggles with his eating habits while on the road. He even pats his ample belly to emphasize the point. Five minutes later, the flight attendant asks if we'd like breakfast. We have two choices: scrambled eggs with cheese and chopped chives, diced potatoes, and sausage, or raisin bran cereal with fat-free milk, yogurt, and a banana. Tony chooses the cheesy eggs and sausage. An hour later, at 8:45 a.m., he asks for a double bourbon on the rocks. Calorie count of his breakfast and drink? I don't know; I count dollars, not calories. However, it was significantly higher than raisin bran and fruit.

Tony is an adult making a simple life choice. But in this case, his life choice goes counter to what he says he'd like to change.

Some people decide to change and act immediately; some just talk.

FRANK

At a full-day seminar, the host organization arranges for a buffet-style lunch. I line up at the serving tables with the 120 participants. I'm near the end and I look down the table to decide what goodies I'll put on my empty plate. Directly in front of me is a seminar participant, Frank, who's carrying too much body weight for his own good. He turns to me and says, "So many tasty choices!" Then he fills his plate with a salad of fresh lettuce, cut vegetables, and a small portion of grilled chicken. As I follow him down the serving line, he tells me how he was diagnosed with Type 2 diabetes the previous year, just a week after his fiftieth birthday. With a smile, he mentions how happy he is that he's already lost more than forty pounds.

Again, here's an adult making a simple life choice. However, it's clear he's acting on his intentions to regain his health and fitness. Some people act; some just talk.

When you encounter people who have a core purpose to make changes in their lives—to act rather than just talk—they set an example to follow. Here's an absolute life truth: Improvement requires you to change the way you've acted in the past—your habits, behavior, and choices at key decision points throughout the day. Change implies action. Not later—now!

It can take *massive sustained action* to change the most stubborn habits. Remember, it took time to create them, and it will take time to get rid of them.

STEP 5: TAKE ACTION

For your life improvement process to work—to enhance what you can, where you are, with what you have—you must *decide* to act, then *do so.* That's it. By following the first four steps of the *Do What You Can System*, you already have action plans for the areas you intend to change. You've identified your support team and other resources, and you have measures of progress in place. All you have to do now is *act on your plan.*

Following are forty suggestions to consider as you launch Step 5 of your *Do What You Can* action plan. Based on my experiences, these suggestions reflect my observations of people who successfully made the life changes they desired. Use these suggestions for yourself. You'll see there are five general suggestions to apply in any area of change you want, followed by five suggestions for each of the seven life areas discussed previously.

As you execute Step 5, constantly find ways to adapt these suggestions to your own situation.

ACTION SUGGESTIONS—GENERAL

1. **Work with what is.** Life changes come easiest when you use the flow of existing processes and energy. For example, in your career, take advantage of your existing skills

as you look for professional growth opportunities. Focus on matching employer needs with those skills you can already deploy. Make sure others know what you can do right now. Communicate consistently and enthusiastically. Frame the thinking of others by saying, "This is what I'm going to do." Then make it happen so they can see your level of commitment.

Leverage available technology, people, and time to speed up your results. Just like a boat in a stream of rushing water, flow with what's already in place and let it speed you along. If you work *against* the existing flow of events, it will consume your energy and wear you down.

2. **Seek help—but know that action begins and ends with you.** Don't wait for others to take action in support of your efforts; go it alone if necessary. That said, it's indeed energizing to share time with people who think in a similar manner, especially in the early phases when you may be struggling to uproot deep habits. Be around people who share your goals and can lend needed perspective during uncertain moments. A good example is joining Weight Watchers to get support for losing weight.

Find people who are already good at what you want to accomplish. Look for ways to learn from them. When in doubt about how to proceed, copy what these successful people do and see if it works for you.

3. **No days off.** You may need to take lots of action to achieve your goals, so be prepared to do so if necessary. Fortunately, the most significant and long-lasting results come from daily attention to small steps that move you forward. Never miss a day in executing your plan once you begin. Cross off items as you complete them. As your day ends (including weekend days), review your progress. Prepare your to-do list for the following day so you can start each

morning with a clear plan. Then you'll fall asleep each evening feeling organized and highly accomplished!

4. **Bring on the "heat."** One sunny summer afternoon in Chicago, I decided at the last minute to go to a Cubs baseball game by myself. Because I needed only one ticket and wanted to treat myself after several weeks of long hours, I bought the best available seat. Ten minutes later, I was directly behind home plate in the second row, surrounded by scouts from other teams with radar guns used to track the speed of the pitches.

    From that vantage point, the field of play was so close, I could look over the catcher's shoulder and watch the pitcher's face. I could clearly see the concentration and intense physical effort a hard-throwing pitcher puts into every throw. No room for halfhearted efforts here.

    That's exactly the level of energy, passion, and "heat" you need to bring to your efforts. Nothing halfway; no settling for mediocre attempts. Your passion will drive you; your contagious effort will infect your support team, coaches, and mentors.

5. **Catch and correct mistakes quickly.** My father once taught me the basics of golf. One piece of his advice applies in all areas of life: *Hit the ball down the middle.*

    Of course, not every action results in a shot straight down the middle toward your goals. Despite your best efforts, you'll end up in the weeds and rough spots wondering, "How did I get here?" (This question is often accompanied by mumbling a rude remark.)

    Each day, you face hundreds of decision points, some more important than others. You think, you plan, you decide, and then you act—sometimes you go spinning off to the side. As in golf, it's necessary to take recovery shots after making mistakes. Yes, they drain time and energy from your efforts to achieve your goals. But fortunately, you can minimize their effect by monitoring your progress, promptly detecting detours, and quickly responding with corrective action.

ACTION SUGGESTIONS—PHYSICAL

Important: If you don't act to maintain and improve the condition of your body, you jeopardize your long-term plans in all other areas of your life—career, family, finances, and everything else you consider important. Your capacity to act, bring passion to your life, enjoy each day, commit to loved ones, and build a positive future depends on your body's capabilities. You must take good care of your body so you can bring into physical existence the visions and plans you've created in your mind. Regardless of its current state, take immediate, sustained action to make your body better able to support your goals.

Follow these five suggestions for sustaining physical wellness.

1. **Eat well.** For most of my life, I ate whatever I felt like eating. Because I was always active, maintaining reasonable weight and good physical condition came naturally as a benefit. Later in life, I met Kris, the woman who became my wife. From a young age, Kris had been conscious of the quality, source, and ingredients of the food she consumed. Despite those efforts, in her early forties Kris developed an aggressive form of breast cancer. No family history, no predisposing genetics, no environmental exposures (that we know of). Kris simply got ambushed.

   Since her diagnosis, she's fought the cancer beast with every tool at her disposal—diet, exercise, sleep, monitoring, medical treatment, optimism, and a heavy dose of common sense in how she spent her time. Her number one weapon is information. Like me, she's an auditor and accountant by training, but she became far more analytical and research-focused than I could ever hope to be.

The cancer spurred Kris to pursue her true passion—nutrition—and she's become a voracious student of the subject. What she's taught me about food could fill many notebooks, even though she only passes along the few details I need to hear to take care of myself. After all, when she said "I do" at our wedding, she was investing in our future. It was time for me to match that commitment in my own dietary behavior. Kris sets the example by her actions; I owe it to her to match her passion about the foods we consume.

You can learn from my bride, too. *Eat well.* Your body needs quality fuel to support your transformation goals. Each time you make a decision about what to eat or drink, take a moment to question the source of the food, *all* of the ingredients, and what's been added during preparation. Research the Internet, library, and bookstores. Look at multiple sources of information to get a balanced report. Avoid those ingredients and foods that slow you down. Emphasize those foods that are good for you. If you don't understand what's in a product, don't buy it. Pay attention and make choices that support your life goals. Parents, make healthy choices for your children and model good nutritional behavior.

P.S. Never pass up broccoli.

2. **Move more.** Exercise fine-tunes your body and makes your internal systems run more efficiently. It flushes out poisons and builds muscle. Just as important, exercise relaxes your mind, stimulates your creativity, and focuses your mental efforts. You don't agree? Get up right now and take a brisk walk for ten minutes. I promise you'll agree that you're more focused when you get back.

A daily habit of aerobic exercise and muscle conditioning will produce noticeable results in just a few weeks. However, many people are legitimately challenged by busy schedules, multiple commitments, and lack of access to a gym or other formal training facilities. Remember the mantra of *The System*: *Do what you can, with what you've got, where you are.*

Here's one of those "no excuses" ideas. Buy an inexpensive but reliable pedometer—a small device you wear that measures the number of steps you take. Reset it to zero each morning, and each evening write down the number of steps you took that day. Initially, keep moving until you reach a higher number than the day before. Remember—no days off! Aim for a target of an hour's walk every day—about three miles at a reasonable walking pace. When you have worked up to that goal, be sure to maintain it. Find a walking buddy—a neighbor, friend, coworker, or family member who will keep you on track with your daily walking plan. Or walk by yourself and use the time to allow your mind to relax and drift. I have some of my best thinking moments in the middle of my brisk walk early in the morning.

(Of course, if it's appropriate for you, get checked out by a physician before beginning any exercise plan regardless of how modest it might be.)

Just get started and exercise as much as you're able, but at least take a walk every day. Right now might be a good time to start. (Go ahead. I'll wait for you right here.)

3. **Get plenty of sleep.** It took me a long time to grasp the importance of sleep. For many years, I believed I could function at 100 percent on five or six hours of sleep as long as I had a sufficient supply of coffee nearby. For most of my adult life, I got to sleep at midnight and was up at five or six, which seemed to work just fine. However, in the mountains of Colorado where I live now, most people turn out their lights by ten. Then, early each morning before the workday begins, the roads and paths are busy with

walkers, bikers, and hikers. Being surrounded by neighbors who were showing me a better way to end the day and start the following morning caused the "aha!" moment that changed my own behavior.

As I look back, it was an easy change for me to make. Here's the formula. Turn off the TV at nine, asleep by ten, up at six a.m. with eight hours of sleep. Bring on the day! Get out and exercise early before the day gets busy and the excuses add up. Afraid you'll miss those favorite late-night TV shows? I have a three-letter solution: DVR.

Give this pattern of sleeping eight hours a try. And when you get up, take that early morning walk before starting your busy day. See if you experience what I did when I made the change—more energy all day long. If it works for you, make it a daily ritual during your work-week. You can always stay up late on weekends.

4. **Get a regular physical examination.** More than a suggestion, this is a must-do item for your action list. Get everything checked, including your eyesight, and keep a record of your results. Research what your blood test and other lab test scores signify: Ask questions of your doctors and their assistants. Establish a baseline for your tests and keep an eye on any trends. Use the Internet and other sources to gather background information. As with nutrition, use a variety of sources to get a balanced view of best practices.

If it's been several years since your last exam, or if you've never had a complete physical, pick up the phone and schedule one right now. As with all areas of your life, take full responsibility for your health. Make the call.

5. **If you smoke, stop. Now.** Don't wait until lung cancer or heart disease strike. Get assistance if you need it. Years ago, little help was available but today, it's easy to find. Why? The death toll, for one thing.

According to the Centers for Disease Control and Prevention, more deaths are caused each year by tobacco than by HIV, illegal drugs, alcohol, motor vehicles, suicides, and murders combined." From the same source, "Cigarette smoking causes about 1 in 5 deaths in the United States each year…On average, adults who smoke cigarettes die 14 years earlier than nonsmokers." Finally, "Tobacco use is the leading preventable cause of death in the United States."[1]

Can you see how much I care about this idea—100 percent preventable death and fourteen additional years of life! I know it's not easy to quit, but you don't have a choice. Under the *Do What You Can System*, you need to be around to accomplish your goals. End of discussion.

ACTION SUGGESTIONS—INTERPERSONAL

It's 8 a.m. Wednesday, March 16, 2011. United Airlines flight 775 from Newark, New Jersey to Chicago O'Hare is scheduled to depart at 10 a.m. No one at the Newark United check-in counter knows where the plane is or when it might arrive or depart. And no one seems to care. Without looking up from the magazine she's reading, the agent points to her right and says, "Go over there to the Continental counter. I'm sure they'll take care of you."

I changed to a Continental flight leaving at 11 a.m. No one mentions that the departure gate is two terminal buildings away. After boarding, the passengers learn that the Continental plane has an oxygen system leak. Mechanics have been working on it for an hour. The pilot announces it should be only a few more minutes while they wait on paperwork. An hour later, after closing the aircraft door, they discover another oxygen leak. The passengers are upset at the lack of communication, let alone that two oxygen system leaks were found on our aircraft. We ask to leave the plane. Still, no one seems to care.

The leaks finally fixed, the plane leaves two hours late. Passengers miss their connections in Chicago. Airline personnel say to go to the Customer Service Center. More than a hundred people are standing in line. Again, no one seems to care.

On another day in another airport, passengers line up for United flight 422 from Denver to the east coast. I'm third in line to board the plane on a busy Monday morning in late March. Several passengers are returning home from Colorado mountain ski vacations. Just as many are business travelers starting another week on the road with this four-hour flight. It's a beautiful morning with sunny skies and a hint of spring in the cool mile-high air. Normal. Routine. Dull. Except for Rufus.

Rufus is our United Airlines gate agent. His job is to take each passenger's boarding pass, scan it, and send us down the people chute. Last year, I took more than 130 flights and don't remember even one of the gate agents. But I remember Rufus.

Rufus is African American. His shaved scalp reflects the overhead fluorescent lighting, and his smile lights up the room. As each of us gives our boarding pass to Rufus, he responds with a hearty welcome and look in the eye. He smiles, shakes each hand, and says, "Have a great week."

Rufus acts as if he actually enjoys knowing that you're flying on his company's airplane. As if he really *wants* you to have a great week—just like he says. Perhaps some people do care after all. This can change a passenger's view of an entire company.

That day, I'm fortunate to be upgraded to first class. (Take 125 flights a year on the same airline and you might be upgraded, too . . . maybe.) I had seat 1D by the window on the left entering the plane. From that position, I can overhear people talking about the wonderful gate agent, Rufus, whom they'd just met.

In this busy world, the one area in which conscious attention greatly affects the quality of life is that of interpersonal skills. People have become increasingly distracted, busy, and self-involved with an absence of civility becoming the norm. They seem afraid of connecting with each other, even making eye contact and offering a smile, and I don't know why. It's a shame. This problem could be fixed for free—but who's willing to tackle it?

Interpersonal skills start and end with your awareness of and respect for every other person you meet. These five action ideas might help as you consider possible changes to how you interact with others.

1. **Become aware of your interpersonal behaviors.** As with all growth areas, improving interpersonal skills may first require breaking old, less-effective habits. It will help your efforts to become more conscious of how you interact with others, participate in meetings, communicate with your spouse and children, and respond to emails at work. You might be surprised to witness in yourself the same irritating behaviors you see in others.

   Unfiltered observation of your own actions is challenging but not impossible. At times each day, observe your behavior—your body language, how you present yourself to others, your eye contact when someone else is speaking, the words and tone you use, and the interest level you demonstrate when others are speaking to you.

   The next best thing to self-observation may be to ask someone you trust and who knows you well to give you accurate feedback. You might even ask several people and get feedback on your behavior.

   To become a model of outstanding interpersonal behavior, take small steps every day to improve. Others will notice and respond in a similar manner. Imagine a world in which people smile at each other, treat each other kindly, and respect each other's humanity. Such changes would transform everything.

2. **Take full responsibility for the quality of your important relationships.** Assume that the quality of your relationships

rests with you. If you sense personality clashes or other communication challenges between you and someone else, take the initiative and do something about it. Don't wait for others to act. You're responsible for improving the situation and removing all barriers to your success.

Think carefully about what you could do to improve a difficult relationship. Research the subject if necessary. Lots of good information is out there to help you. Just type "books on improving relationships" into any web browser on your computer, and you'll be rewarded with dozens of outstanding suggestions to guide your efforts. Be prepared for your next encounter. Hold your ego in check, think of something kind to say, then say it. But don't seek a kind comment in return as it may not come.

Be mindful of your objective to advance toward goals you've set for yourself. How you present yourself, build rapport, and speak and listen, and how and what you write can either help or hinder your progress. It's entirely up to you.

3. **Communicate, communicate, communicate.** Communication is the art of sharing thoughts and intentions with others. Effective, consistent, and clear communication creates understanding and supports action. Tell others your expectations and needs and pay attention to theirs. Say what you intend to have happen and ask for their help and suggestions.

If you're looking for help, effective books on this subject include *Nonviolent Communication: A Language of Life* by Marshall B. Rosenberg, Ph.D. and for business, *The Empathy Factor: Your Competitive Advantage for Personal, Team and Business Success* by Marie R. Miyashiro. The second book uses the process of the first in business settings. Both are focused on communicating needs.

4. **Create and maintain the best image possible.** Examine your appearance. Does it communicate that you care about yourself and how you present yourself to the world? Pay attention to your attitude and the words you use. Are they generally positive, thoughtful, encouraging, kind? Not only will you uplift yourself, but people who can facilitate your success are observing you and you want to put your best foot forward. At a minimum, relax and smile. This alone can be magnetic.

5. **Ask other people about themselves.** One of the easiest ways to build rapport with others is to simply ask them about themselves, and then let them talk without interruption. Resist the urge to turn the conversation back to you. Focus and listen to what they say. Ask follow-up questions; repeat important points; confirm your interest with eye contact and attentive body language.

The purpose of these five tips is not to allow others to dominate your life and walk all over you. Rather, strong interpersonal skills are absolutely required to advance your career, improve the quality of your relationships, and accelerate your progress in all areas of life. Others will help you achieve your goals but not until they understand and legitimately trust you. So work each day on building that understanding and trust through your behavior and communication skills. You'll see results quickly as you work toward your goals. You *can* influence others in an instant.

Michael Jordan is arguably the single best basketball player of all time. For many years, the Nike corporation ran an advertising campaign urging athletes of all ages and abilities to emulate Jordan's dedication. The tagline "Be Like Mike" was the centerpiece of this campaign. Although few people have the skills, energy, and mental drive of a Michael Jordan, you can have the interpersonal skills that Rufus brings to the job every day. Don't worry about copying Michael Jordan. In your daily dealings with others, just "Be Like Rufus."

ACTION SUGGESTIONS—CAREER AND PROFESSIONAL

Chapter Two defined this area to include all activities you perform that fall under the broad category of "work." When you think about your work and your career goals, whatever they entail, it's an especially good time to recall the theme of *The System*: "Do what you can, with what you've got, where you are."

Since the age of fourteen, I've always had jobs that provided an income—from delivering daily newspapers in my Philadelphia neighborhood to operating my present speaking and consulting business. A combination of parental influence, education, hard work, and more than a little luck enabled me to pursue my personal and professional goals throughout my life. I realize how fortunate I am in this regard and that many people haven't had these advantages. Therefore, it's with caution and humility that I offer the following five action steps for achieving your career and professional goals.

1. **Always provide superb service.** No matter what you do in your work, be known as someone who's reliable and always goes the extra mile. Look for ways to separate yourself from others in a positive way—not to discredit *them* but to set *you* apart. Others may be known for providing good service; you want to be known for providing *superb* service. Indeed, get obsessed about the quality of your work. Improve every day—technically, administratively, and personally. Create demand by exceeding expectations.

2. **Build your referral network before you need it.** Make sure others who can help you with your career are aware of your abilities. Build a wide range of supporters. Don't pester them with requests for help, but also don't miss an opportunity to let them know about your career goals and intentions. When the time comes to ask for their help, they'll already be primed. Take steps each day to increase

your visibility. Write, volunteer, and network. The more people know of you and the superb work you do, the more willing they'll be to refer you.

3. **Dress for success every day.** Pay attention to how you look to others. Ask yourself, "Do I look, dress, and act the part I'm playing?" Perhaps more important, do you look, dress, and act the part you would *like* to play—your next job, desired profession, or dream position. Pay attention to your speech patterns, work habits, and energy levels. With regard to your goals, think of the three most important people you'll encounter today. What will they see in you? Is it what you want them to see? Is what they see accurate? Appearances aren't everything, but in business, they're important. When in doubt, press your clothes and shine your shoes.

4. **Plan meetings, conversations, and encounters that can advance your career.** Some people just do what's in front of them each day without concern for planning and learning, much less a view to the future. Perhaps they hope that good fortune will somehow fall in their laps. Is this you? Or do you

- *plan your meetings and interviews;*
- *prepare written meeting agendas as the norm rather than the exception;*
- *come across to others as prepared, insightful, and interesting;*
- *keep meetings on track, on time, and on topic;*
- *present solutions to issues that others haven't considered; or*

- *have the skills and tools needed to present a business case to leaders, including competence in financial spreadsheets, presentation software, business writing, and public speaking?*

   If not, take immediate steps to learn the skills critical to your situation. Take a class. Search the Internet for on-line help. Ask for assistance from others at work or from friends. Show that you're curious and want to learn and others will be pleased to demonstrate their skills to you.

5. **Obtain usable feedback on your performance.** In my experience, getting objective, usable performance feedback in a business setting is extremely rare. Feedback should be specific and concrete, and both positive and negative. If you're not getting it, ask for it from supervisors and others who are qualified to help you improve and show interest in your growth. Don't wait for constructive criticism from supervisors; *demand it!* Ask for details about how you can grow in your job and improve your skills. Remember the advice in Step 4: *Find a mentor or coach.* Make sure you find someone who can and will give you the feedback you need.

ACTION SUGGESTIONS—FINANCIAL

With retirement perhaps a dozen years down the road, I have a gnawing feeling I haven't prepared well enough. In 2011, the world economy is struggling to recover from the financial meltdown of 2008. Throughout parts of the United States, real estate values are nothing short of terrible, and for many people, pensions are a dream of the past. The safety nets of Social Security and Medicare are under attack as lawmakers attempt to address the US federal deficit. Not a pretty picture for those weighing their long-term financial situation or old-age medical care.

As a CPA, not a financial advisor, I have to be careful not to give what might be interpreted as financial advice. Therefore, please don't construe the suggestions below that way. Rather, view them as common sense.

With that qualification, here are five actions I suggest based on my knowledge of accounting and my observation of others who are financially successful.

1. **Protect what you have.** In the same manner that good health is a necessary foundation for transformation, a stable, reliable financial base is critical for long-term personal growth and overall security. Be aware of the financial risks in your life and learn how to manage those risks. Invest in sufficient insurance to cover your health, home, vehicles, belongings, and anything else of value. Build a reserve to cover expenses in case of an emergency. Research what works best from a cross-section of sources. Act today to protect the assets you have.

2. **Save now.** The one regret I carry is failing to begin saving as soon as I started my first job. Had I set aside even a modest amount from each paycheck, I would be much better positioned to weather the inevitable financial challenges that will occur in the coming years. Saving has become my single highest priority.

    Regardless of your age, put aside whatever you can for long-term growth. Follow this simple advice: save, save, and save some more. Then invest your savings wisely and enjoy watching your balance grow over the years. As your accounts grow, research options for long-term investments. Find an investment advisor who can help. Ask friends for referrals or inquire at your bank. Get started on both saving and researching options. Don't put it off. Start now.

3. **Make smart long-term investments.** In decisions involving housing, education, vehicles, and other multiyear investments, take care not to let your emotions overrule your rational self. When you do, you'll enjoy the benefits of your wise decisions without worrying if you can afford them. When making major buying decisions, think through the cash outlay over the entire period of the purchase and your return on its investment. *Always buy within your means.*

4. **Consume wisely.** Closely tied to your ability to save consistently and protect your financial resources is a daily habit of wise consumption. Where you shop, what you buy, how you spend your free time, the frequency you eat out, and hundreds of other routine decisions have a direct effect on your financial stability. Make sure you keep your entire financial picture in mind when you buy. And watch that credit card debt. It can build to unmanageable levels if you're not careful. If you use credit cards, be sure you can handle all the payments and still have enough reserves for your regular living expenses and recreation. Yes, it's all common sense. Do you follow it? If not, start now.

5. **Expand your knowledge of finance and accounting.** Not everyone was put on this planet to become a finance expert or CPA. However, you do need a basic understanding of accounting, cost analysis, taxes, return on investment, and cash flow. Why? To protect your financial resources, make sound investment and buying decisions, manage your household from paycheck to paycheck, and advance your career. You can learn as you go. Ask questions of others who are more experienced in these matters. Experiment with building basic accounting spreadsheets. Make sure you understand the financial information you need for your current job and what you'll require for your next

job (planning, remember?). Don't put it off. A modest amount of study and research throughout your life will pay dividends through better decisions you make, wider career opportunities you find, and a more secure financial base on which to build all areas of your life.

ACTION SUGGESTIONS—INTELLECTUAL

The Intellectual You includes the knowledge enhancement and creative areas of your life. Because my art abilities limit me to producing poorly drawn stick figures, I seek other outlets—speaking and writing, for example. I also love to read, and through reading, I'm constantly learning.

How are you enhancing your intellectual and creative skills? Take a moment and reread the action plan you created in Step 4 that addresses the Intellectual You. In addition to the ideas you recorded, consider the following five general suggestions for daily growth in this area.

1. **Give yourself permission to daydream.** As a child, you likely daydreamed all the time, thoughts wandering off without boundary, creating freely. Then, through the education process and normal life experiences, you pushed your daydreams aside to focus on thinking—to learn how to memorize and apply logic to situations. Perhaps your creativity was discouraged. After all, the ability to repeat information from books is rewarded. Except in certain educational settings, the situation remains much the same today.

   If children can daydream and be creative so naturally, it seems that creativity is a normal capability that gets suppressed through formal education, maturity, and career and family responsibilities. To counteract that, take a five-minute daydreaming break every day. You earned it by being responsible for the remainder of your day! Daydream intentionally. Daydream about what you want to create in your life. That's where everything starts after all—in the mind.

2. **Think for yourself.** This suggestion occurred to me after watching a talking-head television commentator rant for ten minutes about an issue with no consideration of the relevant facts. I'll never waste a minute listening to him again.

In this busy world, you're likely bombarded by programmed messages supporting various products, services, cures, political positions, and hundreds of other issues in the attempt to influence your thinking.

Be careful what you let in to your mind; block the poison and carefully filter everything else. Do your own research on important issues. Listen dispassionately to positions from all sides before making a decision or determining where you stand. Make fact-based decisions. Let me repeat: develop the habit of making fact-based decisions. Resist prepackaged information offered by people and organizations interested only in twisting the truth to support their own agendas.

Every day, practice thinking for yourself.

3. **Develop a pattern of life-long learning.** Make a habit of learning something new every day. Keep your process simple and sustainable. Pay attention for signs of learning opportunities.

For example, without even leaving my chair, three learning opportunities lie directly in front of me. Despite years of knowing that it works, I have no idea how my computer records my keystrokes and converts them to text on my screen. I have no clue how my laptop computer instructs the laser printer to make words and images instantly appear on a piece of paper. Yet it does so with the precision and clarity I would expect from a master craftsman with years of typesetting experience. Nor do I know how the coffee in the cup on my desk gives me just the right jolt to keep writing for another hour. When I focus on it, I realize how little I know—even about the things I touch and use every day in my work. I'm almost afraid to get up and look around!

Be open to learning on any topic, but be sure to focus your limited time and energy in areas that will advance your priority goals. Be open to the concept of having gaps in your knowledge in areas related to your career, finances, physical well-being, and even your spiritual beliefs. Read, research, ask, and learn.

Each day, notice both large and small opportunities to learn something new. Sign up for classes that improve your job skills. Prepare for a new position. Learn a new language, a new game or sport, yoga, or watercolor painting. Use the Internet to get information on a wide variety of topics—such as how computers and caffeine work. Make it a pattern in your day to observe and to learn. Learn intentionally.

4. **Read.** Spending time immersed in an interesting book is one of life's great pleasures for me. The feel of the paper, the visual precision of the words on the page, even the scent from a new or very old book add to the wonderful experience of reading. Reading makes the mind work because it forces the imagination to convert words on a page into images in your mind.

Step away from your computer for at least a few minutes each day and read an old-fashioned book. Stop by your local library or bookstore and give yourself permission to spend fifteen minutes looking around. Don't rush down the aisles; pick one that offers insight in the goal areas you're pursuing. Read the titles on the spines of the books lined up in front of you. Take one or two from the shelf and page through the contents. If the topic looks interesting or helpful, sit down for five minutes and read a half-dozen pages. I did this yesterday at a bookstore in the Denver airport. Ten minutes later, I was on my way with three great books each addressing an area of business growth I'm working on. Total cost: $45.00. Total value: Enormous if I get just one good idea that can advance my business goals. And I got that one idea in the first five pages of the first book. Anything else I learn in the rest of the reading is pure profit!

Get in the habit of reading from a good book every day. You'll exercise your mind, learn something new that will advance you toward your goals, and you may even find something interesting or fun to offer in conversations.

5. **Use Root Cause Analysis.** Root Cause Analysis is used by engineers, quality control managers, business executives, physicians, and others who need to know exactly why something happened. This disciplined thought process analyzes more than just the symptoms of the event (although collecting and studying symptoms is part of the process) and produces more than educated guesses (although listing "what if" scenarios often helps). In Root Cause Analysis, the person or team examining an issue objectively considers *every* possible cause, then tests each one scientifically to determine which need to be addressed to improve the situation.

A brief example: The front end of your car makes a strange grinding sound when you turn sharply to the right or left. Is it a problem with your tires, wear and tear on the steering system, or an indication of a ball joint about to fail? Good mechanics consider all possibilities, test each, and come to a logical conclusion through a process of elimination. In doing so, they use the principles of Root Cause Analysis. They don't make arbitrary decisions about the cause based on beliefs; they test the factual probabilities.

Take a few minutes and research this concept in detail, then creatively apply it to issues holding you back from achieving your goals. For example, is your stalled advancement at work due to your supervisor's preferences, your inability to demonstrate your skills effectively, or your lack of required skills? Learn how to apply Root Cause Analysis to any situation in which you feel your growth and transformation being blocked. Get in the habit of focusing your efforts on the real cause, not just the symptoms. Knowing the true root cause will allow you to address it and take effective action to correct it.

ACTION SUGGESTIONS—SPIRITUAL

Spiritual beliefs are deeply personal. For many, these beliefs are firmly rooted in the culture and customs of specific faith groups. Others put their spiritual beliefs into action more privately.

I encourage you to act in alignment with your higher self, your spirit. To live a spiritual life is to act "in spirit" or in an "inspired" manner, stressing what people have in common—morality and ethics, or beliefs about what's right and what isn't. It includes concepts such as caring for those less fortunate.

People have more in common on spiritual matters than the stories of world or domestic political faith-based conflict would have us believe. As a result, we can accomplish a lot by working together toward the inherent good for all.

With that explanation in mind, I humbly offer these five action ideas.

1. **Examine, know, and own your core beliefs.** Each morning before heading out for the day, take a few minutes to calm your thoughts and relax. Focus on the core foundation beliefs that you want to drive your daily actions and decisions. Allow yourself the luxury of thinking deeply about what's best for you and for others.

Test, refine, and expand your beliefs over time. Read, study, meditate, and ask. Make it a habit to look beyond surface appearances to the deeper levels beneath. Seek to understand *why* you may have beliefs and habits that hold you back, *why* you may treat coworkers and subordinates as an inconvenience, and *why* it's important to care for your physical self and the world around you. In doing so, you become more comfortable with how to align your beliefs and actions.

2. **Act in alignment with your beliefs.** At decision points you face each day, choose the alternative that most closely aligns with your beliefs:

    - *What to eat*
    - *What to say*
    - *What to write*
    - *Whether to exercise*
    - *How fast to drive*
    - *How to perceive the actions of others*
    - *Whether to get out of the chair and take a walk*
    - *Whether to be kind to the person in your life who drives you crazy. . . .*

    Much is written about how leaders should *walk their talk*. I suggest looking for opportunities to *walk your beliefs*. No need to talk about it. Just do it.

3. **Help others.** Every day, act on at least one opportunity to help someone else. Teach a coworker or subordinate how to be more effective. Lend a hand to someone crossing your path who could benefit right now from your actions. Show kindness to strangers, even with just your smile. If

possible, contribute your money, time, or other resources to a charity. At a minimum, help one person every day. Again—no need to talk about it. Just do it.

4. **Share time with others on a similar spiritual path.** Look for people who are seeking a deeper understanding of their spiritual side. Meet with them, listen to their thoughts, questions, and doubts. Find a possible spiritual mentor or coach who's been walking this path for some time and request information, insight, or just conversation. If what you hear resonates with you, consider establishing an ongoing mentor relationship.

5. **Learn from the "angels" in your life.** John Travolta plays the angel Michael in the 1996 movie with the same name. Twenty-five minutes in, the cast is seated around the breakfast table at the small Iowa motel where Michael is a guest. An unshaven Michael, wearing only his full-length white angel wings and workman's overalls, shovels spoonful after spoonful of sugary cereal into his mouth. An inexperienced reporter for a gossip newspaper played by Andie MacDowell offers, "I thought angels were cleaner." After a few lines of conversation covering other angel characteristics like halos and inner light, Michael leans toward her and replies, "I'm not that kind of angel."

I've always enjoyed this scene because I see Michael in many of the angels in my life. No halos or inner light. Not even necessarily tidy. But spiritual guides nonetheless.

To me, an angel is anyone who can help you advance on your path of spiritual growth. My parents are angels who taught me the meaning of dedication, commitment, and respect. My wife is an angel who continues to teach me certainty and unconditional love. My niece Allison taught me about strength as she fought and defeated meningitis while in high school (and went on to be part of a woman's national collegiate championship track team at

UCLA a few years later!). Over a span of 20 years, author, speaker, and spiritual mentor Dr. Wayne Dyer has taught me to ask why, to be open to all things, and to face each day with an optimistic curiosity of "what if . . . ."

Who are your spiritual guides or angels? Take care to observe the higher-level lessons they teach through how they live, then think and act as they do.

ACTION SUGGESTIONS—PSYCHOLOGICAL

How you view the world and process your thoughts is a private experience. Accordingly, my purpose is not to offer mental health advice. Certainly as a CPA, I have no professional qualifications in this area. Rather, I focus on the effective, healthy attitudes successful people bring to their lives. As with all action suggestions in this chapter, the key remains adapting these suggestions to your *own* goals.

1. **Be optimistic.** Successful people lean toward optimism in their beliefs and in their expectations of others, but they're realistic as well. They believe the glass is half full, but also realize the glass probably has some chips, cracks, and other imperfections they must work around. So successful people set aggressive, optimistic goals for themselves and others, but they balance those goals with a heavy dose of reality. After all, setting personal performance targets that are so high they're unattainable is a formula for frustration and failure.

2. **Be peaceful.** Some people are like human tornadoes going through life causing a swirling storm of confusion, uncertainty, missed deadlines, stress, and drama. Often they're so distracted they're completely unaware of the damage in their wake, leaving mess after mess for others to clean up.

    Fortunately, many other people feel at peace in their thoughts, their approach to life, and their interactions with others. Borrowing the words of Henry David Thoreau, these people advance confidently in the direction of their dreams. They take calm, steady action on all their objectives, moving forward toward their goals while reflecting on what they've accomplished and what they still need to do. Their calm attention to detail allows them to act each day in an organized manner. Success in all areas of their life comes in a regular, steady flow.

Have you noticed? Peaceful people are easy to work with and be around because they're aware of how their behavior affects others.

How do others see *you*? Are you like a tornado, like a calm angel, or something in between? If you're peaceful, aware, organized in your thoughts and calm in your interactions with others, you're more likely to get help in achieving your goals than if you're not. And by the way, peaceful doesn't mean an absence of passion. Rather, peace is an inner state that allows optimistic enthusiasm rather than agitated excitement.

3. **Be helpful.** Notice when others could benefit from a moment or an hour of your time. When circumstances are appropriate, kindly suggest ideas that address their challenges. Balance your helpful approach with meeting your own needs. No sense in letting others take unfair advantage of your kindness. Balance is the key.

    Lend a hand at work. Help out in your community. Regularly assist friends and family. Be open to requests from strangers. Most people who benefit from your help will look for opportunities to assist you in return. If you build a reputation as someone who's genuinely helpful, it will pay you back a thousand fold as you pursue your goals.

4. **Give up the need to be right.** When a disagreement is escalating, recognize if you're just trying to prove you're right when it simply doesn't matter. "If I'm right, you're

wrong" seems to be the mantra of far too many people operating in politics, spirituality, education, parenting, energy use, and climate change, to name a few areas of contention. Worse yet, the damaging phrase "I'm right, *therefore* you're wrong!" is the blueprint in dozens of routine interactions involving driving habits, customer service, disagreements with coworkers, and so on.

Accept that you don't need to take advantage of every opportunity to let others know you're right. Especially when tempers rise and deeply held but opposing beliefs are debated, be willing to let go of this need. Just walk away. Allow the facts to emerge in an unemotional, objective manner.

Remember, if a position is factually true, there's no need to prove it. If it's false, then no amount of shouting or arguing will make it true. If a position is based solely on informed opinion and interpretation (politics, for example), then all opinions are "right" and should be respected for what they are. Debates should be enlightening, not punishing.

To be clear, I'm not suggesting you roll over and accept someone else's opinion in place of your own. Rather, I'm saying the need to always prove you're right puts up a barrier to achieving your goals. Any anger you feel limits your effectiveness. Remember where you're headed. *You* defined the destination. *You* created the visualized image of what you would like in your life. Ask, "Does always having to be right help me—or get in my way?"

5. **Seek solutions.** Life challenges are everywhere. A company sells you a poor quality product. A store clerk is rude. A person at the next table in a quiet restaurant speaks out loud on her mobile phone. Politicians blatantly misrepresent facts. Customers complain even though you did your absolute best to serve them.

Problems (and problem people) can consume your thinking. What matters is your *reaction* to them. Can you keep problems in perspective and see beyond the challenging issue of the moment? Can you focus on the bigger picture and seek solutions?

When people complain, ask if they have a solution or suggestion that might help. When the behavior of others has a negative effect on you, politely ask them to be more considerate, or if possible, move away from them. If public figures and broadcasters misrepresent or ignore facts, contact them and point this out. Present the facts and unbiased research that support your position. When companies sell poor quality, let them know—and post your experience on consumer websites. Even if you don't get replies when you reach out, you'll feel better for at least trying.

What if energy prices cut into your limited budget? Fretting about things you can't control will only put you in a psychological tailspin. Look for what you can control and make the changes you can make. Turn off household appliances, lights, and computers that aren't in use. Bump the air conditioner setting up a degree or two in summer and the heat down a bit during cold weather. When driving, slow down to get better gas mileage. Keep your peace and do what you can. It's much easier on your psyche as well as on those around you.

Become known as someone interested in finding solutions— the overall message I want to make. Taking steps to enhance your psychological health provides one more piece of the foundation you need to advance toward your goals in all areas of your life. Be mindful of your thoughts, your reactions, your attitude, and your state of mind. Do what you can, with what you have, and where you are. And do it now.

OVERVIEW OF

CHAPTER FIVE

Step 5 covered the transition from creating your vision and plan (Steps 1 through 4) to executing your plan. You can adopt the suggestions offered in this chapter to support your specific action plans from Step 4. Take action on all parts of your plans, moving forward on your initiatives every day. Be flexible in your approach but firm in your progress. Remember, no days off.

When you encounter a setback or barrier, regroup, rethink your approach, and do something differently. That's the focus of Chapter Six.

MEASURE, RE-ACT, AND MANAGE REALITIES

In Step 4 of the *Do What You Can System,* you created a detailed plan and in Step 5 you put that plan into action. By now, daily action on your objectives should be well underway. You're ready for Step 6, which includes these three distinct but closely related areas needed to ensure your success:

- *Measure your results*
- *Adjust and re-act*
- *Manage realities that affect your progress*

STEP 6A: MEASURE YOUR RESULTS

Dan, a sixty-two-year-old electronics engineer, sat across from me in a small, hot conference room. In July in New Orleans, every room seemed hot. We're both experienced in business practices for companies large and small. Dan's specialty is making complicated technology work for his customers. Mine is making sure that projects like Dan's get done according to authorized plans and completed on time and within budget.

After an hour discussing the results of one particularly challenging project, Dan leaned toward me and, in his wonderful Louisiana drawl, whispered, "The simple difference between us is—I live in a world of reality rather than a world of numbers like y'all do."

A hundred snappy replies ran through my head, but in a rare moment, I said nothing. Instead, I let Dan's statement hang in the damp New Orleans summer air.

Now, the list of really important things I've learned is surprisingly short. It includes "keep your word" and "always double check that what others are supposed to do actually gets done." Right at the top of my list, though, is this lesson: "What we measure tends to improve." Hence, my "world of numbers" has an extremely practical aspect. This is what I stopped myself from sharing with Dan.

In business, setting up and tracking measures of progress are critical to the success of initiatives. In fact, all quality improvement programs are based on measures followed by adjustments followed by more measurement. The same holds true for initiatives in your personal life. The more you measure your progress and adjust to results, the more likely you'll keep moving in the right direction.

Using this logic, it follows that an absence of measures can hold you back. If you lack signposts of progress and can't evaluate the status of your goals, how can you know if your actions are effective?

Measuring progress reinforces your efforts and provides feelings of satisfaction about how far you've come. For example, you'd step on a bathroom scale every week and be proud of the weight loss progress you've made. Or you'd look at your savings account and smile at how much your balance has grown in the last month. Or you'd jog up a flight of steps and enjoy knowing that was impossible a few short weeks ago. Or you'd acknowledge the smiles and compliments from coworkers because you've changed how you interact with them. Yes, you know you're on the right path when your children smile as they see you, when your partner asks you to spend more time together, and when your parents comment on the positive changes they notice in you.

Each evening, sit for a few minutes and review the progress on your to-do list for that day. Take pride in the number of items you crossed off. Enjoy preparing your list for the following morning. These minutes of reflection and planning might just become your favorite time of the day.

Measures come in many forms. Some are *quantitative* and easy to calculate and track, such as financial balances, body weight, and frequency of positive comments from others. Others, such as peace of mind, energy, and happiness, require internally focused *qualitative* measures. I put this one qualitative measure above all others: *How much are you enjoying the change, growth, and transformation you're pursuing?*

Okay, perhaps you don't love every minute or even every day of it. But over time, do you feel joy in the results you're experiencing? Remember your core premise: You're advancing toward your vision of what you really want in your life—by *your* definition. Know this: Progress toward your dreams should bring you joy.

Years ago, I heard Anthony Robbins speak in New Haven, Connecticut. With several thousand people in attendance, his meeting agenda included numerous life-management topics. One of the ideas from that day has stuck with me for more than twenty years—that we must have the "sensory acuity" to "see" ourselves and our actions. That requires being self-aware as though you were objectively watching yourself from across the room, evaluating your actions, and making adjustments so you can get even better results. This isn't to say you need to have an out-of-body experience to evaluate them (although it might help). You simply need a heightened awareness.

When reviewing your own effectiveness, having measures helps you avoid the mistaken belief that you did something better or worse than you really did. Measures also help you objectively observe and analyze your actions—always difficult to do when it comes to your own performance.

To complement your own measures, ask for feedback from trusted friends in your support team. Tell them not to sugarcoat their observations. Instead, ask them to give you the cold hard facts to analyze, adjust, and grow.

To an extent, I agree with Dan the electronics engineer who said, "Reality isn't *all* about numbers." However, numbers certainly have their place when measuring results. Detecting outcomes that differ from your intentions at an early stage lets you adjust your approach and recover quickly. Be open to both hard quantitative and soft qualitative measures.

STEP 6B: ADJUST AND RE-ACT

During one meeting with my business coach, we kicked around ideas on writing, editing, and publishing this book. We brainstormed how long it might take to reach the goal of having the book available in print and electronic reader formats. We also discussed my intention of leading a minimum of twenty-five presentations on the *Do What You Can System* in the first year after publication. From there, we created a timeline for writing, producing, and marketing the book and related material. Then we added seminars, workshops, and keynote addresses to the mix of activities. I told him I wanted to invest one full year in the writing and development phase, then a second year for actively marketing my work. Suddenly, he asked, "And then what?"

"My gut says if this concept didn't fly after two years of intense effort, I'd evaluate continuing it."

Orvel Ray flat-out replied, "John, you're wrong."

That got my attention.

"After two years of trying," he told me, "instead of quitting, you adjust and keep going into year three!"

I realize he was 100 percent correct. And I give the same advice to you. If you believe in a goal, you measure your progress at key points, keep going with what is working, and adjust activities that aren't producing what you want. *Do what you can, with what you've got, right where you are.*

To that I add adjust, push forward, re-act, and don't make yourself crazy along the way. Give yourself permission to pause and stand down every now and then. Make balance and sustainable effort key to your long-term outcomes. Be proactive but flexible. If you're not getting the results you want, try something else.

For example, after two or three months of intense effort on your business goals, build in a week of vacation or other time off. Let your mind and body relax and recharge. Then take a fresh look at where you are and where you want to go before resuming your work. Make the adjustments needed based on your results so far. I make a point of taking a long weekend at home or a few days away every two months to relax and recharge. I may hike or snowboard, watch TV or just sleep late. I look forward to these mini-vacations as a reward for my hard work. And they always give me a fresh perspective as I resume the pursuit of my goals. Remember, the journey toward a goal is meant to be fun.

When you encounter a setback or barrier, take a step back, smile, refresh, and rethink your approach. You're probably trying to undo years of habits while laying down new behaviors that align with your vision and goals. Breaking and replacing behaviors takes time, attention, energy, persistence, and repetition. So give yourself a break every now and then.

STEP 6C: MANAGE REALITIES THAT AFFECT YOUR PROGRESS

In *How Successful People Think,* John C. Maxwell writes, "Reality is the difference between what we wish for and what is."[1] Sounds a lot like Roosevelt's motto: Do what you can, with what you've got, where you are.

As you dream and act big, managing today's and tomorrow's realities is essential. That's why your *Do What You Can* plan requires paying attention to these nine reality-based issues:

Reality #1: Limited Time.

When is there ever enough time to get everything done? Let's face it; time can't be stretched to allow more tasks in your day. Instead, you have to balance your plans to reflect the time available. With an unlimited number of factors to consider, you can let time slip through your fingers.

One recommended strategy is to leave a reasonable cushion around deadlines. Estimate how long it will take to accomplish each of your objectives and then add time "just in case." You can expect something to come up by surprise and slow your progress. Allow for issues that need your immediate attention. Manage your limited time well.

Reality #2: Limited Energy.

The human body can expend only a finite amount of energy before being depleted. If you allow yourself to get completely run down, recharging your physical self will demand your full attention. Achieving the goals you set in Steps 3 and 4 may take five years. Plan for an effort of close to that length of time. Train, maintain, and tune your body as part of your plan. Push toward your goals each day at an intensity level you can sustain over a long period.

Remember, transformation takes energy fueled by sufficient rest, healthy food, and regular physical exercise. Constantly monitor and adjust your energy state. After challenging efforts, take time to recharge that energy supply. Relax and rest as your reward.

Reality #3: Limited Information and Skills.

In pursuing your goals, you likely don't have all the information and skills you'll need. Dealing with reality implies building new information and skills into your plans. The research doesn't end when you set your plans in motion. Realistically assess the information and skills that you lack. And never assume you know all you need to know to achieve your life goals. No one does, especially when starting out. Adopt an ongoing attitude of asking, listening, and learning.

Reality #4: Limited Resources.

With the world's population increasing, we're approaching the limits of clean water, reliable energy, safe affordable housing, effective waste disposal, nutritious food, and reliable transportation and technology. This is true even in developed countries. Indeed, humanity could be facing the biggest challenge in the history of modern man.

While I believe humanity has available what's needed to solve our most pressing challenges, we just haven't seen many of the solutions yet. Until we do, we need to use our limited resources wisely. So as you pursue your goals, tread lightly. Be aware of the ecological footprint you leave behind by what you consume and the waste you generate. Be open to opportunities to consume less and do it more efficiently, to reduce waste-generating purchases and behaviors. Live comfortably but intelligently, with an eye to the effect you have on the environment.

Reality #5: Change.

You're changing, but everything else is changing, too. Your targets and your priorities, your health and your finances, your family and your responsibilities—they all change. As you work toward your goals, you won't be living in a vacuum, so acknowledge that you're chasing a moving target. As you execute your well-researched plan, be ready to adjust it. Avoid getting discouraged when factors you can't control get in the way. Instead, constantly respond to the realities of change with a positive attitude. The challenge of change keeps you on your toes.

Reality #6: Capacity versus Efficiency.

Think of "capacity" as the absolute upper limit of what you can do within a certain timeframe. If you ran full out at 100 percent effort over several weeks, this would give you an idea of your capacity. Efficiency measures your ability to successfully accomplish your goals with minimum effort and waste. The trick is to identify the level of effort that's comfortably below your capacity but still produces the desired effect sustainably.

Like a machine, you can't run at maximum speed all the time or you'll begin to break down and eventually fail. For example, students learn quickly that all-night cramming for an examination can't be sustained. Their clarity of thinking and attention to details suffer. Similarly, working seventy-hour weeks while meeting your responsibilities to your family, health, and peace of mind simply won't work over time. As an example, over the years through sports, I pushed my knees too hard. As a result, I had major replacement surgery and three months of restricted daily activity during recovery. Build into your plan the most efficient level of effort and pursue your goals within that range.

Regarding being efficient, sports such as golf, tennis, or skiing make people aware of the need for recovery activities that include efforts needed to fix a mistake. In golf, this might be the shot you take to get out of the rough and back on the fairway. That shot doesn't move you forward; it gets you back to where you can advance in the right direction. In dieting, it's the extra discipline to recover from an evening of heavy food at a good restaurant. In relationships, it includes what you need to do to make things right between you and your partner, family, friends, clients, or coworkers after you've been neglectful or insensitive.

Yes, recovery activities are inherently inefficient. They waste energy, time, money, and other resources. My knee surgery itself cost me three months of lost income on top of medical bills. Recovery activities can't be dismissed; they're part of all human endeavors.

However, you can minimize the cost of them through careful planning, monitoring, measuring, and prompt corrective action.

Reality #7: Inertia versus Momentum.

Inertia: a tendency to remain in a fixed condition without change; disinclination to move or act. You may not think about change because you're in a comfortable rut, or you may desire to act, but the power of inertia pulls you back. You may want to get up and exercise, but you stay on the couch curious to know what's next on TV. Two hours later, you're still sitting until it's time to go to bed. You may plan to talk with your children or partner but instead stay at your desk and surf the Internet or return emails. Each payday, you intend to put fifty dollars in the cookie jar toward your rainy day fund but forget to do it. Driving home at the end of a long day, you think about lingering after dinner to review accomplishments and setbacks from the day, then write your to-do list for the following day. Instead, after consuming a heavy dinner, you feel lethargic and watch TV for an hour before heading to bed.

Inertia encompasses habits you've accumulated that keep you in your comfort zone. Eating the same fast food. Driving at the same time on the same route through the same traffic. Going through the motions in your job without consciously planning for what comes next. Giving in to inertia requires no thought or energy beyond what you expended yesterday. Be aware of inertia—the enemy of positive change. Fight against its power over your actions.

Momentum: the impetus of a moving object; strength or force that keeps growing

A moving car has momentum; the higher the speed, the more force is required to stop the car. Rockets shot into orbit need immense momentum to overcome the pull of the earth's gravity. Sports teams and political candidates want positive momentum to post their wins. Once they've gathered speed, they work hard to keep the momentum growing.

To generate momentum and build on victories, apply even more effort in the same direction. Develop steam to propel you through moments of indecision by building on a steady list of small accomplishments every day. The more steps you take in pursuit of your goals, the more momentum you gather. The more momentum you build, the easier you can pull away from the inertia of past habits that hold you back.

Imagine the enormous force needed for a large rocket to move off its launch pad. It fights the force of inertia that strives to remain at rest. Once in flight, however, inertia and gravity lessen their hold. Momentum builds until, in orbit, the rocket moves effortlessly at high speed.

In your efforts, expend the energy it takes to break away from inertia to build momentum. Get to your point quickly and efficiently. That's when your own momentum accelerates you out of past habits and into the orbit of transformation.

Reality #8: Friction, Tension, and Stress.

Picture in your mind the force needed to move the earth's land masses even a fraction of an inch, knowing that entire continents have moved hundreds of miles over millions of years. When rocks of any size rub together, friction is created, which results from the tension and stress placed on the surfaces moving against each other. Friction, tension, and stress are natural forces created by change in the physical world—by forces acting against each other as inertia is overcome and movement occurs.

Friction, tension, and stress also occur in the world of personal change and growth. They, too, are the natural result of forces acting against each other as old habits, behaviors, and inertia are overcome and movement toward your goals occurs.

Changing established habits feels uncomfortable at first, which is natural because it's not what you're used to. As an example, a few years ago I switched from skiing to snowboarding. It felt strange. I fell, I stumbled, I made mistakes. But repetition built new skills and habits. Today, the experience of being on skis has faded, but I still love stepping into my snowboard—with my new knees!

For fifty years, I ate nearly anything I wanted in the moment. I wasn't concerned about nutrition or health; after all, I'd never had health problems. Indestructible, or so I thought! But when Kris had a significant life-threatening health scare, she decided to make healthy eating a full-time effort. This directly affected me (a point I'm confident anyone in long-term committed relationships can understand). I read food labels in stores but didn't understand them. I asked questions about ingredients and preparation in restaurants but didn't understand the implications of what I was hearing. For months, the consciously prepared "good-for-me" food tasted different . . . then better . . . and now great. I started with comfort (eating anything I wanted), then I went through uncertainty, tension, and stress (confused over labeling, ignorant about added ingredients and chemicals). Finally, I reached a new level of comfort (ordering and consuming food that's healthy, fresh, and—well—simply food!). As a result, I enjoy eating more, my weight is down, and my daily energy level is higher than ever. Although not perfect, I'm much further along the path of healthy eating than I was five years ago.

Undoing fifty years of habits required conscious daily attention. I often wanted to go back to my old ways and eat something I'd learned wasn't good for me. However, with my wife's coaching and a few years of the new routine under my belt, I'm eliminating unhealthy eating habits and adopting better daily nutritional behavior than in the past.

Recognize that positive change can and should cause friction, tension, and stress. Financial health may require you to challenge your spending and make lifestyle changes. Interpersonal growth requires you to check your ego and focus on others. Professional and career growth requires you to take chances and stand out from the pack at work in a positive way. Intellectual and creative growth requires you to try new things, study outside your comfort zone, and listen openly to ideas and opinions.

Because initially new patterns cause uncertainty, confusion, tension, and stress, identify those negative sources and get rid of them if you can. When you're tense, smile, take a deep breath, and push on, knowing you're headed in the right direction. Keep your eyes on the horizon and the long-term changes *you* have decided to make.

Reality #9: Distractions.

Each of these three barriers to growth tends to pull your focus from the improvement task at hand and needs to be actively managed—or avoided.

- *Rigidity and old thinking.* You'll be tempted to fall back into your customary habits of thinking and acting that have gotten you this far. To move forward, be open to new ways of looking at issues, fresh ways of thinking, and different actions. Rigid attachment to where you're from and what you've done gets in the way of progress. Learn from your past, but don't let it distract you from your goals. Carry forward only those thoughts, patterns, and habits that apply to the future. Drop those that will hold you back.

- *Prejudices and flawed beliefs.* Prejudices include any predetermined opinion (prejudgment) that you bring to a situation. Prejudging people based on their background, race, or beliefs can limit your effectiveness. Even prejudging food, music, and books can limit your ability to learn and grow. Be aware of all prejudgments you make.

  Flawed beliefs are based on inaccurate or incomplete information. For example, buying food or investing your money based on flawed information can slow down your progress in the areas of health and finances. Listening to only one side of a political issue can cause you to vote in a way you might later regret. Consider all angles.

Once you're aware of the potential for flawed or limiting beliefs, base your opinions and actions on fact as much as possible. That way, you'll take informed actions that make movement toward your goals more effective.

- *Inaction by others.* As you pursue your goals, you'll encounter people who simply won't take reasonable action to address solvable problems or avoid them altogether. This shows up in people who take daily actions that damage their long-term health. It also shows up in the dangerous habit of driving too fast or talking or texting on cell phones while driving at high speeds. People who won't address issues, fix mistakes, and solve problems can distract you from your goals. For example, be cautious around family and friends who routinely socialize over large, unhealthy meals. These happy moments can tempt you to deviate from your plans to reduce weight and get in shape. Watch out for coworkers who complain constantly but do nothing about making their work environment better. Also commuters who burn time and energy sitting in traffic every day but won't try a different route or ask about flexible hours or working at home one day a week. Whenever possible, avoid these people and situations. Otherwise, limit contact with them and their effect on your results. Choose instead to be around others who take action to solve problems and get things done.

OVERVIEW OF

In Step 5, you initiated your plan by taking daily action toward what you visualized and defined as your goals. Step 6 reminded you of the following three important issues to consider as you proceed:

1. Measure and monitor your results.

2. Adjust your approach to reflect changing circumstances and remedy results that don't match your intentions.

3. Be aware of and manage realities that can get in your way. This reflects your mandate to do what you can, with what you've got, where you are. You addressed the need to handle

- *your time,*
- *your energy,*
- *limitations on the information and skills you have,*
- *limitations on resources available to you,*
- *change (especially change you have no control over but has a direct impact on your plans),*
- *your capacity to take action in a needed and efficient manner,*
- *results of inertia and momentum on your growth efforts,*
- *effects of friction, tension, and stress that naturally result from change, and*

- *dangerous distractions, including*

  ✓ *being rigidly tied to past thinking and behaviors;*
  ✓ *acting on prejudices and flawed beliefs, not objective facts; and*
  ✓ *inaction by others.*

Beware the temptation to be so focused on rigidly executing your action plan that you fail to give equal attention to measuring, re-acting, and managing realities. Many people have failed to achieve their goals, not due to lack of intention, but for being inflexible when implementing them. Good intentions often break down when execution wavers. Why? People are unwilling to change their plans when necessary.

Pursuing your goals isn't a sprint but a daily effort over time, so be focused but flexible. Measure your progress. Change your approach when needed. And always keep your eye on the intended destination.

The approach of the first six chapters suggested you "do this; don't do that; build on this; leave that behind." In this chapter, I intentionally changed the tone to explain why I feel so deeply about the *Do What You Can System* and how passionately I feel about its ability to help you achieve your goals. It relates to how your efforts to advance toward your *own* goals help to move humanity forward.

What's the ultimate goal for all of us? The creation of a cleaner, more peaceful and positive world.

Here's my way of articulating this ultimate goal: I believe each person has been placed on this earth at this time for a purpose—each one with a unique purpose and all of us collectively. That may or may not coincide with your belief, and that's okay. Beliefs are true for the person who holds them.

I also believe that consistent with one's purpose is a desire to fully explore one's potential as a human being—to become "actualized" (to borrow from philosophers) or to "be all that [we] can be" (to borrow from advertisers). At the core of *my* purpose is helping people reach that potential in their own way.

A lifelong optimist, I believe that if people work together, we can solve the challenges facing our families, communities, nations, and planet. We have the resources and methods available to solve the individual and collective issues we face—poverty, hunger, energy, pollution, clean water, political and religious tension, and more. Granted, we can't see all the needed solutions today, but I believe they're available for us to discover through our collective, unified efforts.

My inherent optimism frees me to explore this two-word question: *What if?* And my biggest question of all is this: *What if large numbers of people move in the direction of individual growth, responsible goal achievement, and positive personal transformation?*

Throughout this book, you've been encouraged to be open to positive change and growth in your life. Let's go to a broader level and ask this: *What if large numbers of people decided to be open and act on these ideas simultaneously?*

For example, *what if* all workers came to their jobs each day with an attitude of pursuing excellence? *What if* they came wanting to help their coworkers be responsive to the needs of their customers and gave their full attention to the tasks involved in their jobs? *What if* all parents—especially fathers—decided they would make their families a high priority by showing their partners and children they loved them through their actions and words? *What if* all of us demanded healthy food, clean water, and safe living conditions? *What if* all politicians and other high-ranking leaders stopped manipulating issues and people for their own gain, and did their jobs the best they could?

Certainly a large percentage of workers, parents, and leaders already act in this manner—but *what if* most did?

These two simple words—*what if?*—represent an enormous challenge.

As you progress toward your goals and transform your life, determine how you might influence others to become more aware of their own effectiveness. Take advantage of opportunities to be an example to them. Stress what you have in common rather than how you differ.

By consistently asking *what if?* through your behavior as well as your words, you can positively influence each person you encounter? The following suggestions show how you might do that.

IMAGINE THESE HIGH-LEVEL *WHAT IFS*

What if we all become more aware of who we are, why we're here on this earth at this time, and how our decisions, habits, and actions might become more consistent with our purpose? *What if* everyone we encounter—even for a few seconds—acted in alignment with that purpose every day?

What if we all become more aware of our impact on this tiny crowded earth? To quote a wise friend, "All of our journeys are off the planet." Hopefully not too soon but very soon indeed when compared to the bigger picture of our existence. After all, we don't own what's here; at best we borrow or rent it during the short time we're here.

What if we all decide to take better care of our planet, to be better stewards of the resources we have for the benefit of each other and all who come after us?

What if we all become more conscious consumers who make it a priority to know the full costs—financial and otherwise—of what we consume, how much we consume, the source of what we ingest or use, and the implications of our buying decisions? Certainly environmental issues are involved, but here I focus on awareness that leads to good health so we can fully enjoy life and take action that supports our goals.

What if we live smarter than ever and when we make choices, we choose the best path in all aspects of life?

131

What if we all become more aware of how we affect others—at crowded events, while driving, in meetings at our jobs, when involved in activities that make noise or put smoke into the air? Who's affected by how we maintain our properties and ourselves, and how we sound to others?

What if we all make less noise, listen more, and be more aware of those who cross our paths each day?

What if we all come to work each day rested and energized, with the intention to perform as well as we know we could? Supervisors and managers at every level: *What if* you focus on helping your staff and employees grow in their jobs? *What if* you teach them not only what they needed to know to perform well today, but what they require to someday replace you and advance through the organization? Employees: *What if* you put aside behaviors that were at odds with what your job requires and instead pay conscious, respectful attention to supervisors, coworkers, and customers, doing whatever you could do to help others every day?

What if politicians and other leaders humbly speak the truth and then act every day in accordance with that truth? That includes advertisers, broadcasters, and media professionals on all sides of every issue. *What if* they present only well-researched, fact-based information to the public, allowing viewers, readers, and listeners to make informed decisions when they purchase, vote, invest, eat, and make hundreds of everyday decisions? And in turn, *what if* we all listen to this fact-based information with an open mind.

What if all adults, and especially parents, model good behavior to children through our food choices and how we maintain our bodies, through our driving habits, the language we use, the respectful ways we treat others, the TV shows and movies we watch and support, and what we read? *What if* we model reasonable spending and diligent savings?

What if we all set an outstanding example of hard work and respect for our employers, coworkers, family members, friends, and strangers?

What if we all honor our responsibilities and do what's necessary to meet the commitments we make?

What if we develop the habit of noticing without judging?

What if we think before we speak?

What if we make a point of being present, of paying attention to what's going on in front of us, rather than being distracted by technology or by planning our next activity, even our next sentence?

Here's a good example. My twenty-six-year-old nephew, Christopher, made a visit to our home a few winters ago. In addition to his snowboard and warm clothes, he brought his laptop computer and handheld phone (he's highly accomplished at texting, emailing, and talking on the phone—often simultaneously). Yet when my wife or I came into the room, he immediately put his technological gadgets to the side and was fully engaged in conversation with us "old people."

A not-so-good example. While I was driving to a client meeting in Denver, I stopped for coffee at a convenience store right off a highway exit. A young girl—my guess is nine or ten years old—came into the store and walked toward where she thought the restrooms would be. All the while, she was focused on the text, tweet, or email she was composing on her handheld device. She walked directly into one adult, then another, then finally into the end of a metal display case, knocking several bags of potato chips to the ground. With each minor collision, she merely backed up a step and proceeded at an angle away from the obstruction until she hit the next one—all without looking up from the screen or offering a word of apology to the adults (or the potato chips). She mindlessly worked her way through the room and, after a few more collisions, found herself in a ninety-degree corner wedged between two floor-to-ceiling refrigerated display cases. Only then did she look up and realize she'd been heading in the wrong direction ever since she entered the store. The whole episode lasted no more than ten seconds, but it brought me an hour of smiles on the rest of my drive to Denver. That said, what isn't funny at all are the patterns of behavior being built at moments like these—patterns that include distraction, lack of attention to the task at hand, and poor social skills. And when this kid starts driving—look out!

What if we all put down the technology, turn off the TV, set aside what we're reading, and fully pay attention to the moment in front of us? *What if* we plan for the future but stay attentive in the present? Our children and coworkers would certainly appreciate it. And so would customers.

Here's an example. I experienced a retail clerk at an office supply chain store texting on her Blackberry with her left hand while ringing up my order with her right hand. I asked her a detailed question about the technical features of an item I was buying while she was engaged in these duel activities. Could she do three things at once? Amazingly, she did. However, a week later, I asked the store manager if she still worked there. He said he had to let her go because she kept making mistakes.

What if honesty, truth, diligence, enthusiasm, fairness, sound ethics, and a commitment to our responsibilities ruled all actions for every one of us? *What if* our standard was "excellence" rather than "good enough"? *What if* we all ask, "How could I do this better?" And then did it?

What if we stop fighting? At home, in our neighborhoods, at work, in politics, and even between nations. Just stopped.

What if we all simply choose peace over conflict? *What if* instead of paying the huge cost of supporting conflict, we invest an equal amount in service to each other? To feed, clothe, and protect those in need, to save and invest, to reduce the enormous individual, family, and national debt that will hold us all back for years to come?

What if we all stop giving energy to what we honestly don't believe in, to what we've proven doesn't work, to what other people tell us we should do with our lives? What if we stop listening to the spin-doctors and the one-sided talking heads, start doing our own research on important issues, and begin thinking *intentionally* for ourselves?

What if, instead, we emphasize *what we can do, where we all are, with what we all have in common?*

What if we all stress finding solutions rather than creating or continuing problems?

If all of these *what ifs* actually happened, could we even imagine what our lives would be like?

You can make your own decisions, as can I. But while personal improvement comes from intentional *personal* action, massive improvement comes from massive *group* action. I honestly believe the solutions to humanity's greatest and most insignificant challenges can be realized if enough people decide they are critical—and take action accordingly.

PURSUE YOUR GOALS WITHIN THE CONTEXT OF THE WORLD

Known for his written opinion pieces that looked at American life with a critical eye, H. L. Mencken was a journalist, editor, and writer for five decades up to 1948. One of my favorite Mencken quotations is, "Any man who afflicts the human race with ideas must be prepared to see them misunderstood." I really enjoy this tongue-in-cheek view of expressing one's ideas in public, so if you disagree, let the emails and letters fly. It's all part of being self-aware.

Perhaps you're sitting with jaw dropped wondering why I'm deviating from concrete goals, fact-based actions, and quantifiable measurements with this *what if?* daydreaming. One answer: to demonstrate that a number-crunching auditor/accountant can have a thoughtful, introspective side. Another answer: to attempt to balance and integrate individual goals with the needs of others and the world. After all, it's important to pursue your goals (the trees) in the context of the world in which you operate (the forest).

Yes, it's wise to back away from your current focus and take a long, thoughtful look at the big picture—my overarching intention here. I encourage you to consider the powerful *what if* potential of what could happen if we set and implemented goals that benefited the whole. In aiming to influence large numbers of people to pursue their distinct purposes, if we all did so with vigor each day, our collective positive energy would create a massive "human improvement movement."

That's as transparent as I can possibly be. I hope you want to be an active part of the movement I'm calling the *Do What You Can Revolution*! There's no club to join, no card to carry, no secret handshake—simply take your daily actions toward your positive purpose.

Imagine *what if* we all do what we can, right where we are, with all that we have?

What if . . . ?

CHAPTER SEVEN

Starting in 1989, Vaclav Havel was president of Czechoslovakia (1989-1992) and of the Czech Republic (1993-2003). For years prior to this time, Czechoslovakia was under the oppressive influence of the Soviet Union. Before his election in 1989, Havel was an activist for political change as well as a scholar and poet. In one of his often-quoted statements, he said, "Hope is not the conviction that something will turn out well but the certainty that something makes sense, regardless of how it turns out."

What a powerful statement—and a life lesson to us all.

This chapter asks you to balance *your* planning against wide-ranging *what if* questions that affect everyone. That means in the process of setting intentions, goals, and actions, make sure they reflect truth, civility, and respect for yourself and others. Act with "the certainty that something makes sense, regardless of how it turns out," as Havel once said.

It also asks you to dream big. Integrate your grand goals with those that people worldwide could share with you. And through your example and outreach, you'll encourage others to do the same.

CHAPTER EIGHT

MAKE
IT SO!

It's the first week of June. Spring finally arrived on Monday in Colorado's Rocky Mountains. Summer followed on Wednesday. From subfreezing temperatures and snow to eighty degrees and green grass in a matter of days. Such is the weather here.

As I sit in the sun and catch up on paperwork, I find a recent issue of *Time* magazine in my stack of mail. The cover story: "The Science of Optimism: Hope isn't rational so why are humans wired for it?" This excerpt from the lead article (based on a book titled *The Optimism Bias* by Tali Sharot) states:

> You might expect optimism to erode under the tide of news about violent conflicts, high unemployment, tornadoes and floods and all the threats and failures that shape human life. Collectively we can grow pessimistic—about the direction of our country or the ability of our leaders to improve education or reduce crime. But private optimism, about our personal future, remains incredibly resilient.[1]

I love that phrase—private optimism—because it expresses a key concept of this *Do What You Can System*. Further, from the same article:

> To make progress, we need to be able to imagine alternative realities—better ones—and we need to believe that we can achieve them. Such faith helps motivate us to pursue our goals.[2]

My *what if?* ideas and philosophy fit right here. I feel "privately optimistic" as I express what I believe in my core—that all people deserve the opportunity to advance confidently in the direction of their dreams (as Thoreau has said). Our past is our foundation, the present where we are now, and the future is the alternative reality that we can imagine, pursue, and make real.

I've attempted to make the *Do What You Can System* real by listing twenty action points in the section that follows. These points recap the six steps I advocate. Indeed, I've executed each one for myself as I wrote out the *Do What You Can System*.

TWENTY POINTS FOR PURSUING YOUR PURPOSE

In the television series *Star Trek: The Next Generation*, after deciding on a course of action, the captain of the starship Enterprise would give the command "Make it so!" What a simple yet powerful statement. It means take action and cause it to be—no misinterpretation, no debate.

I've summarized the twenty key points of the *Do What You Can System* here and issue you a challenge to "Make them so!"

1. **Identify and Pursue Your Purpose.** You're here on this earth at this time for a purpose. Identify it and formulate a

plan to live in harmony with it. Fully explore your potential and help others do the same.

2. **Do What You Can, Could, and Must.** Doing what you *can* was your starting point in the *Do What You Can System*. Doing what you *could* aligns your individual responsibilities with the collective needs of the whole. Doing what you *must* with whatever you have, wherever you are, aligns you with your purpose.

3. **You are 100% Response-Able.** Over the long run, you're 100 percent responsible for the goals you pursue and results you achieve. Others who care about you will help, but ultimately, getting the results you want is up to you.

4. **Your Past is Your Foundation.** Be aware of where you're from and the strengths, abilities, and weaknesses you bring from your past. They serve as your foundation for growth, your jumping-off point. Although your past will always be there as a reference point, you needn't let it define who you are now or where you're headed. Leave behind barriers, limitations, and distractions. When you do, you can carry forward what will help you grow.

5. **Know Where You Want to Go.** Focus your thoughts. Think intentionally. Visualize the end point of your growth efforts. Color in the details. Force yourself to take time to sit and think. As Henry Ford said, "Thinking is the hardest work there is." Do the hard work of defining where you're headed before you set out. On a regular basis, stop, look, and think again. Match your skills with your goals and fill in any gaps with deliberate action.

6. **Write Out Your Plans.** Write out your objectives, resources, needs, time schedule, action steps, and measures. Build a written, integrated, structured plan of action—one that's open to flexibility. Well thought-out plans are efficient; acting on impulse isn't. If it's not written out, it's not a plan.

7. **Change Requires Work.** Uprooting deeply held beliefs and habits requires conscious, focused, intentional action over time. To overcome inertia, build momentum, and sustain new directions takes lots of energy. Change requires work.

8. **Use Daily To-Do Lists.** Break your dreams down into actions you can take today. Every day, write out exactly what you will do that day in pursuit of your goals. Be specific. Work that list with vigor. Smile as you cross off completed tasks. Enjoy the feeling of accomplishment. At night, review your results for the day and prepare your list for the following day. Repeat this process every single day. No days off.

9. **Change Causes Stress.** Change—your past rubbing against your future—will likely cause stress, tension, and friction in your life. These are natural reactions to change. Manage any stress your changes cause in yourself and others. Most of all, expect stress, acknowledge it, feel it, and manage it.

10. **Chop Wood, Carry Water.** Remember the following Zen saying regardless of your beliefs, background, or spiritual foundation: "Before enlightenment; chop wood, carry water. After enlightenment, chop wood, carry water." Along with your personal growth, your grand goals and great dreams, you must also tend to what needs to be done. Be present with your everyday duties.

11. **Manage Your Limits.** Acknowledge that other people have the skills and knowledge you need. Seek them out and ask for help. Offer them something of value in return. Maximize your ability to leverage and multiply your efforts through information, coaches, mentors, and a support team.

12. **Bring the Heat.** Passion fuels the fire of change—your passion for what is important to you. Avoid halfhearted efforts. This requires you to determine what you *are* passionate about and to focus on it.

13. **Do Good Work.** Give your best to your employers, your employees, your coworkers, your family, and all others who cross your path. Surprise them with your abilities. Others are entitled to your best, and so are you.

14. **Seek Truth.** Make truth, honesty, and sincerity critical values in your life. Don't just accept the statements of others; make a habit of finding out the facts. Working with fact-based information and decisions is essential for achieving your goals.

15. **Take Care of Yourself.** Mind your body. If it breaks down, your progress comes to a screeching halt. Seek healthy fuel to keep it going. Exercise to keep it tuned properly. Get adequate rest so it can heal and recover. Tend to your physical well-being, for without it, you put achieving the growth you desire at risk.

16. **Help Others.** You have something to offer other people. It may not be riches or weeks of donated time; it could be a smile, a compliment, a minute to listen, or a suggestion that may help. Serve where you can with what you have. Seek opportunities to help others.

17. **Tread Softly.** Be aware of the effect you have on everything around you—other people, the space you occupy, the resources you consume. Limit the waste you generate. Avoid being an unnecessary burden on others. Spread calm and peace in your wake and leave the world a better place.

18. **Be Congruent.** Be cautious of what thoughts you allow and beliefs you form because they translate into action. Instead, bring your thoughts, beliefs, and actions into harmony. Make sure your actions are congruent with your ideals. Be aware of how you express and present yourself to others.

19. **The Goal is Better, Not Perfect.** This point has been in the background holding all other points together. Your goal in

any transformational initiative is to take action in the right direction for you—to improve, not to become perfect.

20. **Breathe Deeply and Smile.** If you're following this six-step *Do What You Can System* (or a similar initiative), congratulations! You get it! Don't forget to look at your results, however modest or grand, and give yourself a pat on the back. Each day at least once, breathe deeply and smile as if you have a secret. Others will wonder what you're up to; you decide if you want to tell them. As Teddy Roosevelt said:

> The credit belongs to the man who is actually in the arena, whose face is marred by dust and sweat and blood; who strives valiantly, who errs and comes up short again and again…but who knows the great enthusiasms, the great devotions, who spends himself for a worthy cause; who at best knows in the end the triumph of high achievement, and who at the worst, if he fails, at least fails while daring greatly, so that his place shall never be with those cold and timid souls who know neither victory nor defeat.[3]

YOUR ACTION PLAN FOR THE LONG HAUL

Fight to know the challenge of high achievement. See your plans through to completion and spend yourself in your own worthy cause. In Step 2, you set an arbitrary five-year time horizon. Stay with it until you've completed what you set out to do. Make it so!

Any worthy initiative admits the possibility of failure, both during planning and execution. Don't let your visions, good thoughts, and deep desire for growth fall to the wayside due to being discouraged or distracted and failing to follow through. Plan for the long haul. Maintain yourself, build your team, find the right resources, and stay at it.

Follow the example of my father and mother. Through more than sixty-five years of marriage, they got up each morning, clear in their purpose, and happily did what had to be done. They did everything they could, with all that they had, right where they were. Like them, you'll accomplish great things by being clear about what you want, and then taking consistent steps in that direction every day.

Be free to think. Be confident to act.

May you find peace and joy in pursuing your vision. And never—*ever*—pass up broccoli.

RECOMMENDED

"MUST READ" CATEGORY

Switch: How to Change Things When Change is Hard, Chip Heath and Dan Heath ("This is the most informative, useful how-to book I've read in years."—John Hall)

"SHOULD READ" CATEGORY

Eye of the Storm Leadership: 150 Ideas, Stories, Quotes, and Exercises on the Art and Politics of Managing Human Conflicts, Peter S. Adler

How Successful People Think, John Maxwell

Nudge: Improving Decisions About Health, Wealth and Happiness, Richard H. Thaler and Cass R. Sunstein

The Checklist Manifesto: How to Get Things Right, Atul Gawande

The Optimism Bias: A Tour of the Irrationally Positive Brain, Tali Sharot

The Tipping Point: How Little Things Can Make a Big Difference, Malcolm Gladwell

"WHEN YOU GET A FEW FREE HOURS" CATEGORY

Callings: Finding and Following an Authentic Life, Gregg Levoy

Influence: The Psychology of Persuasion, Robert B. Cialdini

RECOMMENDED READING

Nonviolent Communication: A Language of Life, Marshall B. Rosenberg

The 7 Habits of Highly Effective People: Powerful Lessons in Personal Change, Stephen R. Covey

The Empathy Factor: Your Competitive Advantage for Personal, Team and Business Success, Marie R. Miyashiro

Your Erroneous Zones and *Excuses Begone,* Wayne W. Dyer

ACKNOWLEDGMENTS

So many people to thank. At the top of the list is—

My bride Kris, who continues to teach me about love, certainty, and the importance of taking good care of myself.

My coach Orvel Ray Wilson, without whose help and encouragement this book would still be a two-inch-thick mess of unorganized Post-it notes, torn-out articles, and barely readable scribbled messages.

My world-class "get it out the door" team headed by Karen Saunders of MacGraphics Services: Barbara McNichol (editor), Patrice Rhoades-Baum (branding and website content), Kerrie Lian (book layout and cover design), Lauren Klopfenstein (website design and development), Joyce Jay (cover photography), and Helena Mariposa (proofreading and ebook conversion). I recommend this team to anyone considering their first or fiftieth book project. Contact me at John@JohnHallSpeaker.com and I'll connect you with these experts.

Peter S. Adler, PhD, for showing me how to bring patience and a solutions mindset to even the most difficult problems of society. Peter's book *Eye of the Storm Leadership: 150 Ideas, Stories, Quotes, and Exercises on the Art and Politics of Managing Human Conflicts* (www.eyeofthestormleadership.com) should be required reading for leaders in all organizations but especially in politics.

The Beloved faith community at Old Saint Patrick's church in Chicago, especially Terry Nelson-Johnson, Big Ed and Carmel Rita Moore, counselors and confidants Laura Field and Pam Devereux, and many more. Thanks for helping me turn an important corner.

Father John S. Cusick, who renewed my faith in faith one cold Chicago Sunday morning with the simple in-

ACKNOWLEDGMENTS

struction: "Do good work this week." Amen, Father John. (And don't give up on the Cubs.)

My hundreds of clients and coworkers plus many thousands of seminar and workshop participants who, during the past thirty-five years, have trusted me with their attention, ideas, frustrations, and creative solutions.

My anonymous teacher and coach, Dr. Wayne W. Dyer. A three-minute private conversation at a program he led in 1992 changed everything for me!

ENDNOTES

CHAPTER ONE: STOP, LOOK, AND LISTEN

1   Chip Heath and Dan Heath, *Switch: How to Change Things When Change is Hard,* (New York: Crown Business, 2012), 22.

2   Dr. Wayne Dyer, *Your Erroneous Zones: Step-by-Step Advice for Escaping the Trap of Negative Thinking and Taking Control of your Life,* (New York: Harper Perennial Edition, 1991), 51.

CHAPTER TWO: DEFINE YOUR HORIZON

1   Dr. Wayne Dyer, *Excuses Begone!: How to Change Lifelong, Self-defeating Thinking Habits,* (New York: Hay House, 2011), 124.

2   John C. Maxwell, *How Successful People Think: Change Your Thinking, Change Your Life,* (New York: Center Street, 2009), xiii.

CHAPTER THREE: FILL IN THE DETAILS

1   Heath, *Switch,* 53.

2   Ibid, 56.

3   Stephen Covey Website; "The 7 Habits of Highly Effective People, Habit 2: Begin with the End in Mind," www.stephencovey.com.

CHAPTER FOUR: CREATE YOUR ACTION PLAN

1   Ketti Briggs, *Look Homeward Angel* (stage script), (New York: Samuel French Inc., 1958), 5.

ENDNOTES

CHAPTER FIVE: TIME TO ACT

1   Centers for Disease Control and Prevention, www.cdc.gov/tobacco/data_statistics/fact_sheets/ health_effects/ tobacco_related_mortality.

CHAPTER SIX: MEASURE, RE-ACT, AND MANAGE REALITIES

1   Maxwell, *How Successful People Think*, 38.

CHAPTER EIGHT: MAKE IT SO!

1   Tali Sharot, "The Science of Optimism: Hope isn't rational so why are humans wired for it?," *Time* magazine, June 6, 2010, 41- 42 (Excerpt: Tali Sharot, *The Optimism Bias: A Tour of the Irrationally Positive Brain*, (New York:Pantheon, 2010).

2   Ibid.

3   Theodore Roosevelt, "Citizen in a Republic," speech at the Sorbonne, Paris, April 23, 1910.

ABOUT THE AUTHOR

John J. Hall, CPA, is an author, speaker, and results expert who presents around the world at conventions, corporate meetings, and association events.

Throughout his thirty-five-year career as a business consultant, corporate executive, and professional speaker, John has helped organizations and individuals achieve measurable results. He continues to inspire audience members in corporations, not-for-profit organizations, and professional associations to step up, take action, and "do what you can."

A sought-after motivational keynote and workshop speaker, John balances his demanding travel schedule with extended stays at home in the Colorado mountains where he and his wife Kris enjoy biking, hiking, snow-shoeing, and snowboarding.

For more information on the *Do What You Can System* or to sign-up for our newsletter, webinars, interactive blog, podcasts, and other materials, visit www.JohnHallSpeaker.com. To contact John or schedule him for your program, use the Contact link or email John@JohnHallSpeaker.com.